OUTLAW TALES

of Oregon

True Stories of the Beaver State's
Most Infamous Crooks, Culprits, and Cutthroats

Second Edition

Jim Yuskavitch

TWODOT®

GUILFORD, CONNECTICUT
HELENA, MONTANA
AN IMPRINT OF ROWMAN & LITTLEFIELD

A · TWODOT® · BOOK

TwoDot is an imprint of Rowman & Littlefield and a registered trademark of Rowman & Littlefield.

Map © Rowman & Littlefield

Distributed by NATIONAL BOOK NETWORK

Library of Congress Cataloging-in-Publication Data

Yuskavitch, James.
  Outlaw tales of Oregon : true stories of the Beaver State's most
infamous crooks, culprits, and cutthroats / Jim Yuskavitch. — 2nd ed.
      p. cm.
  Includes bibliographical references and index.
  ISBN 978-0-7627-7263-6
  1. Outlaws—Oregon—Biography—Anecdotes. 2. Frontier and pioneer
life—Oregon—Anecdotes. 3. Crime—Oregon—History—Anecdotes. 4.
Oregon—Biography—Anecdotes. 5. Oregon—History—Anecdotes. I. Title.

  F876.6.Y87 2012
  979.5'01—dc23

                                                        2012022959

Printed in the United States of America

To my mother, Peg Yuskavitch,
who always encouraged me to pursue the
things that interested me and to never give up.

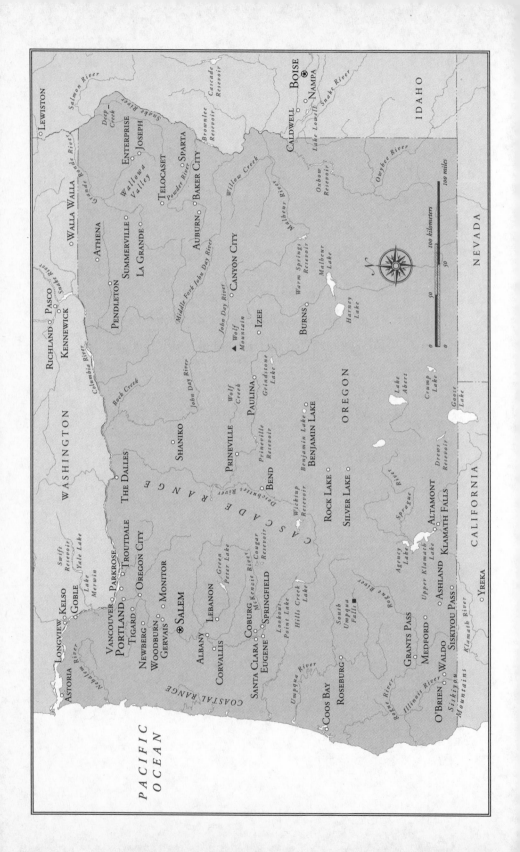

Contents

Acknowledgments vi

Introduction viii

The DeAutremont Brothers 1

The Prineville Vigilantes 15

Black Bart 30

Range Wars 41

Bill Miner 52

Harry Tracy and Dave Merrill 65

The McCartys 78

Dave Tucker 91

Hank Vaughan 100

Incident at Chinese Massacre Cove 112

Carl Panzram 121

The Triskett Gang 136

Bibliography 149

Index 153

About the Author 158

Acknowledgments

Any project of this nature inevitably requires the help of researchers and others knowledgeable in the field of history. This book is no exception. I would like to thank some of the people who helped me find historical information and photographs, gave me valuable advice, or pointed me in productive directions.

Gordon Gillespie, director of the Bowman Museum and the Crook County Historical Society, along with assistant director Steve Lent, provided me with access to their archives and came up with some great historical photographs for use in this book as well. Gary Dielman, professional historian and curator of the Baker County Library, provided photographs, background on local outlaws, and some valuable perspectives on historical research.

Jan Wright, a researcher at the Southern Oregon Historical Society, went out of her way to provide me with some excellent sources on outlaws from her part of the state, as did Denine Rautenstrauch, director of the Enterprise Public Library, who located some especially valuable research material that I would likely not otherwise have procured.

Martha Metcalf, of the Josephine County Historical Society; Ann Hayes, curator of the Wallowa County Museum; Jayne Primrose, curator of the Grant County Historical Society; Connie Nice, coordinator of the Hood River County Museum; and Cate Culver, Calaveras County Historical Society historian, all kindly scoured their archives to find specific photographs I was in search of. Todd Shaffer, reference archivist at the Oregon State Archives, did particularly prodigious duty locating historical photographs for me, as did his colleague Austin Schulz.

Last, but not least, I am indebted to the many authors, popular and scholarly, who have written on the subject of Oregon's outlaws and the state's frontier history. You will find them credited in the bibliography.

Thanks to all of you.

Introduction

Outlaws have been around since there were laws to break. While no reasonable person condones or admires crime and criminals, the highwaymen, bank robbers, train hijackers, and gunfighters of the American frontier West have always held a special iconic spot in our history. Perhaps it's because the outlaw, riding the open range, doing as he pleased and going where he wanted to go, represents in some way a sense of freedom that we aspire to but find increasingly difficult, if not impossible, to attain in today's society.

The Wild West was also the last chapter in our history when the bad guys could be remade as good guys. In their time they were often regarded as Robin Hoods of sorts, fighting the evil stagecoach or railroad monopolies in defense of the put-upon farmer and homesteader. In the myth the outlaws rode into town, robbed the bank, and galloped off in a cloud of dust and a hail of gunfire to their hideout in the hills to plan their next escapade. Some were lionized in the dime novels that were popular at the time.

Oregon had its fair share of these lawless characters, famous and obscure, some of whom you will meet within these pages. While some committed their crimes mainly or wholly within Oregon, all wandered to other states and regions as well, in search of additional criminal opportunities, on the run from the law, or both. But, however interesting their tales may be, the reader will find that the story of most outlaws usually ends badly.

One of the most interesting conversations I had while researching this book was with a Baker County historian who expressed skepticism that I would be able to find out a great deal of authentic, accurate information about a certain outlaw who ran amok in his county in the 1890s. He explained to me that outlaws usually kept their activities to themselves and traveled quietly so as to attract as little notice as possible.

He could not have been more right. The first thing anyone researching this subject will find is the suspect nature of many historical sources on outlaws of the Wild West. Contemporary newspaper stories about outlaws and their depredations are a mix of facts, conjecture, editorializing, and a good bit of embellishment. Historical and contemporary treatises commonly tell different variations of the same event, and even eyewitness accounts often contradict each other.

Into this murky historical pool the researcher wades, trying to make sense of it all and to divine which version of the tales is "most true." I've listened to those voices from the past tell their versions and pondered the ruminations and interpretations of present-day scholars. Out of that mix of fact and myth come my tales of Oregon outlaws. I hope you enjoy them.

The DeAutremont Brothers
Oregon's Last Train Robbery

When Southern Pacific Railroad Train Number 13 came to a slow stop a little before 1:00 p.m. on October 11, 1923, in Tunnel 13 on the summit of Siskiyou Pass in southern Oregon, the eighty-plus passengers aboard must have thought it odd. They only had a few minutes to sit in the darkness and wonder what was going on before a huge explosion rocked the front of the train, breaking out windows on the passenger cars and sending a bright flash of light and billowing, thick smoke through the tunnel.

Conductor J. O. Marrett, assuming a boiler explosion, tried to calm and comfort the panicked passengers as best he could, then stepped out of the car into the black, smoky darkness of the tunnel and carefully began to make his way to the front of the train. It would be some minutes before he realized what the forward crew members already knew—that a brutal and vicious robbery was in progress.

Chugging south to San Francisco, California, Train Number 13 had originated out of Portland, Oregon, and was carrying, in addition to paying passengers, twenty deadheading railroad employees and was pulling four baggage cars.

Tunnel 13 is located just south of Ashland in the Siskiyou Mountains, a remote and wild place in those days. The steep, winding grade through the mountains to the tunnel required additional "helper" engines to get trains to the summit. Just before reaching the tunnel, the trains stopped at Siskiyou Station where the helper engines were unhooked. Then, because the ride down the other side of Siskiyou Pass was also steep and a train could gain four or five miles per hour extra speed before reaching the tunnel, company policy required its engineers to conduct a brake test, slowing down the train before reaching the east end of Tunnel 13 on its way down the mountain. It was all a routine, except for today.

On this day, three brothers—nineteen-year-old Hugh DeAutremont and the twenty-three-year-old twins Roy and Ray DeAutremont—were waiting for the train to reach the tunnel. They were out to make a big, one-time heist that would set them up for a life of leisure, forever free from financial worries. Rumor had it that Train Number 13, called the Gold Special because in past years it transported gold between Portland and San Francisco, was carrying forty thousand dollars in cash on this run.

Now, hidden in the brush along the tracks, Hugh and Roy, armed with Colt .45 automatic pistols, waited at the east end of the tunnel where the train would enter, while Ray, clutching a 12-gauge automatic shotgun, positioned himself at the west entrance.

Their plan was simple. The train, having conducted its brake test before entering the 3,100-foot-long tunnel, would be traveling slowly enough for Hugh and Roy to hop aboard. They would then make their way to the engine car cab and order the engineer to stop the train with the engine outside the exit end of the tunnel and the rest of the train inside. Ray, waiting with his shotgun at the tunnel exit, added extra firepower if needed. They would then blow open the mail car door with dynamite, uncouple the rest of the train, and order the engineer to pull the mail car out of the tunnel, where they would take its valuable cargo, and then disappear into the rugged mountains as rich men.

An hour earlier they had run wires from a detonator hidden in the woods to the tracks and stashed a suitcase filled with

Ray, Hugh, and Roy DeAutremont.
Oregon State Archives

dynamite in the bushes so that everything would be ready to go. The brothers had stolen the explosives and accessories, ironically, from a Southern Pacific Railroad Company work site. Everything was in place, and now all they needed to do was wait for the train to arrive. They had planned it out so well that nothing could possibly go wrong.

The DeAutremonts were not an atypical family for that time period in American history. Ray and Roy were born on March 31, 1900, in Iowa, and Hugh in Arkansas in 1904. They were the middle children in a family of five brothers. Their father, Paul, was of French extraction and their mother, Belle, German. They were Catholics and regular churchgoers.

A barber by trade, the father also tried his hand at farming and ranching and owned a general store for a while. In addition to Arkansas and Iowa, the family also lived for a time in

Colorado and New Mexico. Eventually Paul and Belle divorced, and he moved to Eugene, Oregon, to work as a barber.

Following in their father's footsteps, Roy and Ray moved to Oklahoma to attend barber school, but Ray did not care for the profession and jumped a train one day and rode the rails to Portland, Oregon, arriving in 1918.

While Roy remained in Oklahoma and opened his own barbershop, Ray became involved in the labor movement, specifically with the Industrial Workers of the World party. In November 1919 he was arrested, which was not an uncommon practice for harassing labor activists, and sentenced to one year in a Washington State reformatory on charges of "criminal syndicalism."

Roy came to Oregon when he heard about his brother's arrest, and upon Ray's release, the two lived together in a Salem apartment, scraping by on what work they could find. Some scholars of the DeAutremont case believe that this was a radicalizing period for the two brothers, with Ray's anger and bitterness over his arrest eventually affecting Roy as well.

Ray took off for Spokane, Washington, in 1921 to find work and then went to Chicago where he hoped to join up with "gangsters." Failing to make a connection, he returned to Oregon by the end of the year and hooked up once again with Roy.

The twins, who were always close, began talking about pulling off some major heist that would permanently solve all their financial problems—an idea that first occurred to Ray when he was serving his reformatory sentence from 1919 to 1920. In 1922 the two even went so far as to plan several bank and general store robberies in Oregon and Washington, casing the locations but backing out at the last minute.

Over the next year the brothers spent time with family in Oregon, attended church, and worked at a number of jobs.

Then Ray hopped a train during the winter of 1922–1923 and went to visit his younger brother Hugh, who was attending high school in New Mexico, where his mother Belle remained after her divorce. It was here that he pitched to Hugh the idea of helping him and Roy with a holdup, suggesting that the younger brother come up to Oregon after he graduated.

When Hugh graduated in June 1923, he headed up to Oregon to join Ray and Roy, and they began discussing a plan to rob a Southern Pacific Railroad mail car. Their date with destiny was drawing closer.

The brothers began exploring the Southern Pacific Railroad's route from Portland to northern California, looking for a promising ambush location. But the three just weren't finding a place they liked until Ray remembered Tunnel 13 and the Siskiyou Summit, over which he had traveled on his way to visit Hugh in New Mexico. Their spot was chosen, and they began to plan the details for a late October robbery of the Gold Special.

They went to Portland in early September 1923 and bought a used Nash car, which they drove to Eugene, where their father lived, taking the opportunity while passing through Oregon City to steal the explosives, detonator, and wire they would use in the robbery.

They visited with their father for a few days, then loaded the Nash with camping gear and other provisions and departed on September 18, telling him they were going hunting in Washington's Puget Sound area. Then they turned south, down the Pacific Highway to the Siskiyou Mountains.

Just a little below the summit of Siskiyou Pass, they pulled off the road and concealed the car. Here they camped for about a week, and then moved to another site not far away to spend a few days practicing setting up the explosives and getting familiar with handling their weapons. They did a good deal of target shooting. They also burned their tent and other belongings that might be used to identify them if discovered by the authorities before relocating to a small cabin they found on nearby Mount Crest.

They stayed here for the better part of a week, making their preparations for the robbery, for which they had set a date of October 11.

Next, they sent Hugh to get the car with orders to drive it back to their father's house in Eugene, store it there, and then hop a train for a lift back to the Siskiyou Summit. Because of the very limited road system in the area, attempting a getaway by car would almost certainly result in capture by the authorities. The plan, instead, was for Roy and Hugh to hide in the mountains once the robbery was successfully completed. Ray would make his way back to Eugene, pick up the car, then come and retrieve his brothers and the loot. At that point they would be free to make their escape.

But things went wrong. On the way down the mountain on September 26, Hugh crashed the Nash into a cow that was loitering in the road, crunching in the touring car's front end. He made it into Ashland where he got it repaired, but had to spend a couple of days in town while the work was being done. He finally pulled into Eugene on September 29, leaving the car at his father's house and hopping a train to Ashland. While hanging around the Southern Pacific Railroad yard waiting for a train to come by so he could hitch a ride to the Siskiyou Summit, Hugh was questioned by suspicious security guards. Although they let him go, the episode unnerved him. Instead of waiting for a train and risking getting caught, he hiked up to the Mount Crest cabin from Ashland, reuniting with Ray and Roy on October 9.

The appointed day finally arrived. At noon the brothers set out from the cabin on foot for Tunnel 13. In addition to their weapons, they carried with them the detonating machine wrapped in a pair of blue overalls, three backpacks to carry away the loot, three pads that had been soaked with creosote that they would strap to their feet to confuse bloodhounds, a one-pound can of pepper for the same purpose, flashlights, and a suitcase containing sticks of dynamite.

Upon reaching the tunnel, they attached the wires from the detonator and hid the suitcase by the tracks. Hugh and Roy made their way to the east tunnel entrance. Ray hefted his shotgun, sat down at the west entrance, lit a cigarette, and waited.

But now the waiting was over. The brothers could hear the train approach, slowing down enough during its brake test to allow a person to leap aboard as it passed by. Just before the train entered the tunnel, Hugh and Roy emerged from the brush and swung themselves onto the engine car.

Hugh stole up on engineer Sidney L. Bates and fireman Marvin L. Seng. With pistol drawn, Hugh ordered that the train be stopped with the engine outside the west end of the tunnel and the remaining cars inside. Roy watched from the back of the engine car by the oil tank.

As the engine emerged from the tunnel and the train came to a halt, Ray suddenly appeared, brandishing his shotgun. Mail clerk Elvyn E. Dougherty opened the door of the mail car to see what was going on. When he poked his head out, Ray fired his shotgun, but missed. Dougherty quickly slid the car door shut and locked it. Hugh Haffney, in the baggage car, was also peering out his car door. Seeing what was transpiring, he, too, slid his car door closed and locked it.

Now the DeAutremont brothers had everything under control and everyone where they wanted them. All that was needed now was to blow the door off the mail car, grab the forty thousand dollars, and make clean their escape. The high life was in their grasp.

Ray and Roy went up to the engine cab where Hugh was covering the engineer and fireman. They ordered both trainmen to get down off the cab and marched them out the tunnel to the front of the train where they would be protected from any debris thrown by the explosion they were about to set off.

They placed the suitcase of dynamite by the mail car door, attached the wires, and ran for cover as Roy rammed down the detonator plunger.

But the robbers had no experience using explosives and used far more dynamite than the job required. Instead of just blowing off the door, the explosion tore apart poor US Postal Service mail clerk Elvyn E. Dougherty and virtually demolished the mail car. Baggage man Haffney, in the next car over, was knocked unconscious by the blast.

Immediately after the explosion, while conductor Marrett was still attending to the passengers, brakeman Charles Orin "Coyle" Johnson jumped from one of the rear cars onto the tracks and made his way through the dark smoky tunnel to see what had happened, holding a red lantern to light his way. Rail accidents including derailings and boiler explosions were not unheard of— between 1890 and 1905 there were as many as seven thousand such incidents in the United States. That is probably what Johnson was expecting to find. Instead, he ran into Roy DeAutremont.

The brothers now had a dilemma on their hands. The plan called for uncoupling the mail car from the rest of the train so the engine could pull it out into daylight. At that point the trio could search it until they found the forty thousand dollars they sought. But the explosion filled the tunnel with smoke and flames, making it difficult to see and breathe. They brought fireman Seng back to uncouple the car, but he was overcome by the fumes and had to retreat. Now there was a problem. Then the brakeman blundered into Roy's clutches.

Roy told him that that it was a robbery and demanded that Johnson help uncouple the mail car. The brakeman explained that once the uncoupling lever was raised, the engine had to be moved forward to separate the cars. So Roy sent Johnson forward to tell engineer Bates, who was being covered by Hugh and Ray, to pull the engine and mail car out of the tunnel. But when the brakeman suddenly appeared out of the smoky tunnel, red light in hand, Ray and Hugh panicked and opened up on him with both pistol and shotgun. Johnson fell to the ground, dying. One of the two DeAutremonts, it's not known who, shot Johnson one more time to finish him off.

Now Hugh brought engineer Bates back into his cab and ordered him to pull forward. Unfortunately for the brothers, the mail car had been so badly damaged by the explosion that, even after several tries, it wouldn't budge.

Stunned at how badly things were going, the brothers examined the smoldering carcass of the mail car, strewn with the body parts of the mail clerk, and considered their options. The mail car was so hot and smoky that, in their estimation, by the time it was safe to go inside to loot, the law would probably have arrived on the scene. It looked like it was time to cut their losses.

Roy and Ray held a brief consultation on what they should do. They decided to kill the engineer and the fireman and run for it. Roy shot the fireman two times with his Colt .45. Ray climbed up into the cab of the engine where Hugh was still guarding the engineer and yelled to Hugh, "Bump him off and let's clear out of here."

Hugh shot Bates in the head with his handgun. Then the three brothers ran off into the forest, leaving behind four dead men and the empty backpacks they had brought to fill with stolen cash.

By now the conductor J. O. Marrett had made his way to the mail car accompanied by a medical student passenger, twenty-three-year-old Lawrence E. C. Joers, who had offered to help with anyone who might have been injured in the explosion. Finding their way to the front of the train through the dense smoke, they discovered the engineer, brakeman, and fireman lying on the ground. Still thinking they were only injured from an accidental explosion, the medical student began to give the engineer artificial respiration. But as he applied pressure to the chest, blood spurted out, revealing gunshot wounds. Now it dawned on them that there had been a robbery and multiple murders. Joers soon found the detonating wires along the track. Marrett ran for an emergency telephone located outside the tunnel and called for help.

Before long, another train steamed up the grade carrying a doctor and law enforcement officers who collected evidence. Within hours search parties were combing the area, but no sign of the robbers could be found. Southern Pacific Railroad immediately offered a reward of $2,500 for their capture.

In the wake of the bungled robbery attempt, the three DeAutremont brothers hightailed it to a cache where they had stored some supplies for their escape. They holed up there for nearly two weeks. After what seemed like an adequate period of lying low, Ray borrowed Roy's handgun (Ray had lost his during the robbery) and jumped a train to Medford, intending to continue on to Eugene to retrieve the Nash.

But as Ray walked through town, much to his horror, he spotted a newspaper with pictures of himself and Roy under the caption, "Have you seen the DeAutremont brothers?" There was a $14,400 reward being offered for them dead or alive. That was enough for Ray, who returned to the hideout to tell Roy and Hugh that the law had identified them as the killers.

Now it was time to run and run hard. The three made their way through the mountains toward the coast. By early November they were on the Klamath River in California where Ray decided to strike out on his own while Hugh and Roy continued moving south to Grenada, California. Here, Roy took a job on a farm, and Hugh kept moving.

Unbeknownst to the three brothers, a massive manhunt that included searches on foot, with bloodhounds, and by airplane had been launched. Wanted posters were also being distributed worldwide. Nevertheless, it would be three and a half years before the Tunnel 13 killers would be brought to justice.

The robbery had been such a disaster—the murder of four men and a price on their heads without a penny to show for it. What other mistakes had they made that enabled their names to be connected to the crime so quickly?

The investigating officers found a wealth of evidence at the crime scene and at the cabin on Mount Crest. But two pieces of evidence gave them most of what they wanted. For one thing, the serial number of the handgun that had been dropped at the crime scene identified its purchaser as Ray DeAutremont. But the best evidence came in the form of the coveralls that the brothers had used to wrap up the detonator. Authorities bundled it up and sent it to Professor Edward Heinrich of the University of California at Berkeley. He conducted a series of forensic tests on the garment, but his best results came when he simply looked into one of the pencil pockets and found a wadded up piece of paper. He

Hugh DeAutremont.
Oregon State Archives

unfolded it carefully. It was a US Postal Service registered mail receipt number 236-L for a letter sent by Roy DeAutremont to his older brother, Verne, who was living in New Mexico.

From those two pieces of evidence investigators were quickly able to piece together the robbery plot. Hugh was eventually linked as well through handwriting analysis of the aliases he had used at hotels and from the purchases he had made of equipment used in the robbery attempt.

On November 23, 1923, six indictments were issued against the brothers—four counts of murder and one count each for attempted burglary and larceny. More than two million wanted posters were printed and distributed worldwide. The three-year manhunt would cost five hundred thousand dollars.

While on the lam, Ray ended up in Detroit. He was eventually able to contact Roy in California, who joined him there in 1924. They worked their way south, intending to eventually escape the country. Instead they ended up in Ohio where Ray got married and had a baby girl. In early 1927 Roy and

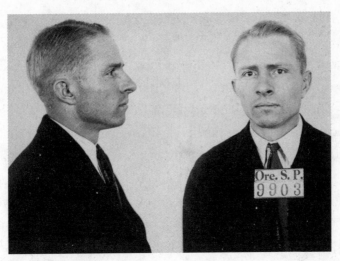

Ray DeAutremont.
Oregon State Archives

Ray went to Steubenville, Ohio, to look for work as coal miners. But the law was closing in. Ray saw a wanted poster of the three of them with Hugh's picture marked as "captured."

After Roy and Hugh had split up in California, Hugh traveled through the Southwest for a while and then journeyed to Chicago. In Chicago he joined the US Army in April 1924 under the name James C. Price. He was assigned to duty in the Philippines.

But the Philippines were not far enough away for Hugh to hide. Before too long the authorities' massive wanted-poster distribution campaign was finally going to pay off. In late 1926 Price's sergeant, Thomas Reynolds, was in San Francisco and saw one of those posters. He immediately recognized Private Price as Hugh DeAutremont. Reynolds took a stroll over to the Southern Pacific Railroad office and told his story.

There had been many false leads and disappointments over the years in the manhunt for the DeAutremonts, but the agents thought this might, finally, be the real thing. They sent one of their men to Manila in February 1927 to check the story out.

By mid-March the agent was back in San Francisco with Hugh DeAutremont in custody. By the end of the month, Hugh DeAutremont was transferred to the custody of Ralph Jennings, sheriff of Jackson County, Oregon, where the crime had taken place.

Three months later an agent from the US Department of Justice arrested Ray at his house in Steubenville. Later that day, local police officers nabbed Roy as he was leaving work at a mill.

The two brothers had been fingered by a former coworker who had recognized their pictures from a wanted poster. It was over.

On June 27, 1927, the three brothers were delivered to the Oregon State Penitentiary in Salem to begin serving life sentences. While serving his time, Hugh founded a prison magazine called *Shadows*. Roy worked as a barber, and Ray learned several languages at the prison school and became a modestly talented painter.

Hugh was paroled in early 1958 and moved to San Francisco to work as a printer. Less than three months later, he was diagnosed with stomach cancer and died on March 30, 1959. Roy was diagnosed with schizophrenia, transferred to the Oregon State Hospital, and given a lobotomy. He was eventually paroled and died in 1983 in a nursing home in Salem. Ray was paroled in 1961 and worked part-time as a janitor at the University of Oregon. He died in 1984.

It was years after their robbery attempt that the DeAutremont brothers learned that Train No. 13 carried only its usual cargo of mail on that October day. There was no forty thousand dollars aboard. It was also Oregon's last train robbery.

The three brothers are buried next to their mother at Salem's Belcrest Memorial Cemetery. All three of their names are on a single headstone inscribed side by side, just as they were on those wanted posters so many years ago.

The Prineville Vigilantes
The Murderous Reign of "Judge Lynch"

On August 18, 1887, a small notice appeared in the Boise, Idaho, *Tri-Weekly Statesman* accusing one Frank Jordan of Harney Valley, Oregon, of being a cattle thief. It warned him that if he did not leave the area, "we will hang you with your own rope." The notice was placed by "Vigilance No. 101." Three years later, the Harney County census showed no resident named Frank Jordan living there.

In the far-flung and remote frontier communities of eastern Oregon, where lawmen were few, it was not especially rare for local folks to take matters into their own hands when they found themselves and their communities beset by lawbreakers.

Those vigilante committees were not ineffective. With rope, gun, and threats, they were often able to eliminate the worst criminal elements in their midst. In fact, there are more than thirty documented cases of hangings by vigilante groups along the Idaho to Oregon gold trails between 1863 and 1865 alone, attesting to the popularity of freelance frontier justice.

Mr. Jordan of Harney Valley should have considered himself lucky. Many troublemakers on the Oregon frontier were not offered the option to get out of town. And vigilante justice was often a gruesome sight. Consider the case of Spanish Tom, who was lynched in the rough-and-tumble eastern Oregon mining town of Auburn in November 1862.

Spanish Tom, also called Tom the Spaniard and known to be a "desperado," stabbed two men to death during the course of a card game argument and then fled town. A few days later he was arrested and returned to Auburn and put under the custody of the sheriff to await trial. But an angry crowd soon gathered, and despite the sheriff's best efforts, Spanish Tom was dragged down the street in his shackles, and a rope was tied around his neck. By the time the mob actually hoisted him into the tree, he was already dead. In the course of the shooting melee that accompanied the lynching, one member of the crowd was killed and two wounded.

While many considered such actions justified on the wild frontier, whenever vigilantes took the law into their own hands to become sheriff, judge, jury, and executioner, they risked becoming outlaws themselves.

That's exactly what happened in Prineville, when, for two tense years, vigilantes ruled. Begun under the guise of protecting citizens from lawlessness, the Prineville vigilantes soon turned their committee into a quest for power using intimidation and violence.

Prineville, established in 1871 and located in the high desert of central Oregon, had a reputation as the "toughest town east of the Cascades," largely because it was a center of the cattle industry and bustled with the hard customers that business attracted. The fact that the county sheriff's office was more than one hundred miles to the north in The Dalles meant Prineville did not get a great deal of law enforcement attention.

Most people say that Prineville's vigilante days began on March 15, 1882, when Garrett Maupin—whose father had helped kill the Paiute war chief Paulina fifteen years earlier—galloped into town to announce that two settlers, A. H. Crooks and his son-in-law, Stephen Jory, had been shot dead. Maupin was traveling in the Grizzly Mountain area north of Prineville and came upon the two bodies. Some accounts claim that he heard the shots that killed the two men and went riding over to investigate, glimpsing Lucius

Langdon, who owned the ranch adjacent to Crooks's property, galloping away from the scene of the crime.

Langdon and Crooks had been feuding for some time over their property lines. Langdon, whose ranch stretched along Willow Creek, had claimed, under the Homestead Act, a forty-acre piece of land that Crooks and Jory believed belonged to them. On that mid-March day Crooks and Jory went out onto the disputed forty-acre tract and began blazing a fence line. Since the two men were working only a couple of hundred yards from Langdon's house, Langdon heard the sound of their axes and rushed over to confront them. He warned Crooks and Jory, who were about to break for lunch, that if they came back they had better come armed.

Taking Langdon at his word, the men returned after eating to continue their work, this time packing revolvers. Langdon confronted them again. Guns were drawn and Langdon was the quicker. With both men lying still on the ground, Langdon mounted his horse and lit out for his brother's cabin, twelve miles away on Mill Creek.

By that time, Maupin had brought news of the murders to town and a posse of about a dozen men formed a "vigilance committee," led by local rancher Bud Thompson, to look for Langdon. Anticipating that the fugitive would probably go to his brother's place, the posse made that their destination, arriving late at night. But Langdon heard them coming and escaped on horseback.

The next day a party of volunteers led by Jim Blakely, another local cattleman, rode out to Langdon's ranch. His group found him at home and arrested him without incident. Langdon, who had fled from the vigilance committee, was content to be taken into the custody of trusted acquaintance Blakely who would turn him over to Deputy Sheriff J. L. Luckey in

Prineville, Oregon, 1881.
Bowman Museum and Crook County Historical Society

Prineville where he would presumably be safe. He was soon to find out how wrong he was.

As Langdon was led away, his hired man, W. H. Harrison, asked to come along to make sure his boss was treated well while under custody. The posse agreed. Rumors had been flying that Harrison had participated in the murders, but since he had been seen in Prineville at the time of the shooting, his alibi was iron-clad. Nevertheless, arrest warrants had been issued for both men.

Back in town, Blakely and his men turned Langdon over to Deputy Sheriff Luckey, who put him in shackles and escorted him to the Jackson House Hotel. Harrison came along as well. In the hotel lobby they made a roaring fire in the stove and tried to get some sleep.

By the time Blakely turned Langdon over to the deputy sheriff, it was close to 2:00 a.m. As Blakely turned toward home for some shut-eye, he noticed a number of local men hanging around the hotel. He thought it looked a little suspicious but never suspected what was coming.

At daylight the ringing of the school bell reverberated through town, sending its message to Prineville's residents that something of importance had happened. The night before, as Deputy Sheriff Luckey was settling in by the stove to guard Langdon through the rest of the night (assisted by Deputy Marshall W. C. Foren), townsfolk had begun wandering in out of what Luckey thought was just morbid curiosity.

Luckey was still warming himself by the fire at 5:00 a.m. when the hotel door flew open and he was knocked to the ground and held there with his eyes covered. Immediately, a half dozen pistol shots rang out and someone groaned. Next, he could hear the cries of Harrison as he was taken from the room.

When Luckey was allowed to rise from the floor, he rushed over to Langdon, finding him dead. At each door of the hotel stood an armed and masked man making threatening gestures so that no one attempted to leave the room. When the masked vigilantes satisfied themselves that Langdon was dead, they vanished into the morning twilight.

When it was light enough to see, a search party led by Luckey went out looking for Harrison. They soon found him— hanging from a beam on the Crooked River Bridge.

The killings of Langdon and Harrison may not have been an entirely spontaneous occurrence. Some believe that a standing vigilance committee had been secretly formed the previous year and was already structured and organized by March 1882.

The vigilantes were ostensibly organized to protect the region's residents from outlaws and especially to battle cattle rustlers and horse thieves. Because the county was still being politically and administratively organized, vigilante committee members soon found a vacuum they could fill to their benefit.

The leader of the vigilante committee was a man named Colonel William "Bud" Thompson, a veteran of the Modoc Indian War, former newspaper owner in Roseburg, killer of at least three men in gunfights, and now a Crook County rancher.

The vigilantes struck again on December 24, 1882. Al Swartz, who was known to be critical and defiant of Thompson and his gang, wandered into Burmeister's Saloon for a Christmas Eve card game. Knowing he had dangerous enemies, he sat down at a card table facing the saloon door. Unfortunately, that put his back to a window. At about 10:00 p.m., an unknown gunman standing outside fired a single shot through the window into the back of Al Swartz's head, killing him instantly.

Further spreading their Christmas joy, a group of vigilantes went that same night to the Barnes Ranch and grabbed two young men who were bunking there—Sidney Huston and Charles Luster. The vigilance committee took them onto the open range, hung them from a juniper tree, then shot them both while they dangled.

Newspaper accounts, relying on information provided by vigilante sympathizers, accused Huston, Luster, and Swartz of being members of an outlaw gang of rustlers and horse thieves. Many citizens doubted that story. Swartz likely drew the vigilantes' ire for his loud public condemnation of the lynching of Harrison. Rumor had it that Luster was killed because he had won a local horse race that the vigilantes had demanded that he throw, betting on himself and crossing the finish line first instead. Huston was probably just in the wrong place at the wrong time.

But that was the whole idea of the vigilantes—to intimidate the local populace so they could eventually run the

Jackson House Hotel where Lucius Langdon was murdered and W. H. Harrison was abducted by the vigilantes.
Bowman Museum and Crook County Historical Society

county by influencing elections, bullying judges and juries, and placing their people in important government positions. All who attempted to defy the vigilantes would find themselves the recipients of a warning in the form of a note featuring skull and crossbones.

In December 1882 the vigilantes also established a "stock association" with bylaws and a constitution that required all cattlemen in the county to register with the association before running their cattle on the open range. A notice to that effect was sent to all area ranchers.

Shortly afterward, Huston, Luster, and Swartz were murdered and accused of being outlaws. The message to ranchers was clear—refuse to do what we say and you may end up just like them.

Two months earlier, on October 24, 1882, Crook County had been officially established, carved out of the much larger

John Luckey, deputy sheriff during the Langdon killing.

Bowman Museum and Crook County Historical Society

Bridge over the Crooked River where Harrison was lynched.
Bowman Museum and Crook County Historical Society

Wasco County. A government structure had been put in place, the county seat based in Prineville. This newly formed county was about 8,600 square miles in size and was home to about 2,600 residents.

The vigilantes had managed to use their influence by intimidation to gain political power. They even had the ear of Governor Z. F. Moody, who had appointed a number of vigilante-affiliated people to high county positions. Their numbers included Colonel Thompson's brother, S. G. Thompson, as county judge, and Gus A. Winckler, a storekeeper who was involved in the Langdon-Harrison murders, as county treasurer.

The new year of 1883 dawned, but the killing was not yet over. Another man, Steve Staats who, like Swartz, would not let the vigilantes push him around, had the top of his head blown off near Powell Butte. Soon after, a rancher named Shorty Davis disappeared, and his body was never found. The vigilantes were suspected in that killing as well.

In the spring of that year, a former employee of vigilante leader Colonel Thompson named Mike Morgan was playing cards with rancher Mossy Barnes at the Dick Graham Saloon. Barnes suddenly accused Morgan of owing him six dollars. When Morgan hedged on paying up, Barnes drew his revolver. Morgan doubted out loud that Barnes would shoot. Barnes quickly proved him wrong by putting a bullet into one of his lungs.

Morgan staggered out of the saloon clutching his chest and walked unsteadily across the street to retrieve his gun, which he had left in the livery stable. Grabbing the weapon, he started back toward the saloon but collapsed on the ground. Before he died six days later, he swore that the gun Barnes had used to shoot him belonged to his old boss and leader of the vigilantes, Colonel Bud Thompson.

The success of the vigilantes and their stock association seemed assured and their power complete. Their people practically ran the newly minted Crook County and were feared enough by its populace to minimize most dissent. Those who were foolish enough to challenge the vigilantes often ended up being carried "feet first" up cemetery hill.

But sooner or later there is a breaking point, when people, no matter how frightened they are, can no longer look the other way. That day came on December 18, 1883.

On that day, Frank Morgan was standing around in Kelly's Saloon talking with friends. Frank's brother, Mike, had been shot earlier in the year with a gun purportedly belonging to vigilante leader Bud Thompson (who, by implication, had ordered the murder). Frank had been going around town promoting that theory.

This wasn't the kind of thing Thompson wanted people saying about him. Standing with his back to the saloon door, Frank Morgan didn't see Thompson stroll into the saloon. The

William Thompson, head of the vigilantes.
Bowman Museum and Crook County Historical Society

vigilante leader quietly approached Morgan, put his revolver to the back of Morgan's neck, and pulled the trigger. Morgan fell to the floor, already dead. Thompson continued to fire into his lifeless body until his gun was empty. Just to make sure the other saloon patrons got the message, he bashed in Morgan's skull with the butt of his pistol.

There was a trial but, since the vigilantes controlled the courts, Thompson went free.

The murders of the Morgan brothers in the same year and Thompson's subsequent acquittal for what was obviously cold-blooded murder were too much even for the cowed residents of Crook County. The murderous reign of the vigilantes and the corrupt justice of "Judge Lynch" had to end. But who would lead them to drive this lawless force from their communities?

For the past two years, standing in defiance of the vigilantes had been a dangerous course of action for any man. Harvey Scott, editor of the *Portland Morning Oregonian* and nemesis of Bud Thompson, had written that anyone marked for death by the colonel was as good as buried.

But not everyone who challenged the vigilantes went out feet first. One of those men was Jim Blakely, who had brought in Langdon and had then been horrified by his and Harrison's murders. When the vigilantes' stock association issued orders demanding that cattle ranchers register with them to use open rangelands, Blakely, who was running cattle fourteen or fifteen miles out of Prineville, responded by placing an order of his own—for two Colt six-shooters and three Smith & Wessons. He gave these to his range riders, and the vigilantes never bothered them.

When county treasurer Gus Winckler remarked to some friends that if Blakely didn't butt out of the vigilantes' business he would end up dead, Blakely strapped on his revolver, confronted the vigilante Winckler, and ran him out of town.

Jim Blakely came from an Oregon pioneer family. His father, Captain James Blakely, had arrived in Oregon Territory in 1846, served in the Rogue River Indian War of 1855–1856, and died in 1914 at the age of 102.

Blakely had been raised in the saddle, helping his father drive cattle between California, Nevada, and Oregon before settling in central Oregon. By 1882 when the vigilantes were just beginning to become active, Blakely was running a cattle business on the rangelands outside of Prineville and was a well-known and respected citizen.

The only way to beat the vigilantes, who were well organized, was to create an equally well organized opposition. So Blakely, along with fellow vigilante opponents John Combs, Sam Smith, T. Clay Neese, and two other men named Stuart and Pett who owned a local gristmill, got together and formed the Citizens Protective Union. They promptly set about the business of convincing the good citizens of Prineville and Crook County to back them up.

Before long the union was eighty strong and had picked up the nickname "Moonshiners" because the group kept watch at night when the masked vigilantes did most of their dirty work.

The final showdown came in the spring of 1884 when the Moonshiners paraded down Prineville's main street in a show of force while a group of vigilantes watched from Til Glaze's saloon. As they passed by that establishment, Blakely shouted out a challenge—if the vigilantes wanted to continue ruling Crook County, they had better come out now and fight for it. Blakely's invitation was greeted with silence. The Prineville vigilantes knew their day was done.

Jim Blakely.
Bowman Museum and Crook County Historical Society

On June 2, 1884, Crook County residents held their first election. The vigilantes were driven out of power and many Moonshiners were elected to public office. Jim Blakely was elected county sheriff. With the power of the law behind him, Blakely soon divested Crook County of its worst lawbreakers, taking special satisfaction in breaking and scattering the vigilantes.

It's not really known how many people were officially vigilantes and vigilante sympathizers, but townsfolk knew or suspected who most of them were. With their power broken, many just went back to being law-abiding citizens. Others came to a bad end. Mossy Barnes committed suicide. Charley Long and George Barnes were killed in gunfights.

But the fear the vigilante era had put into the residents of Crook County lasted for decades, and townsfolk were reticent to talk about the period while its players were still alive—well into the 1940s at least.

Vigilante leader Thompson left Crook County for Alturas, California, where he worked as the editor of the *Alturas Plain Dealer* and was suspected of inciting some vigilante activity in that area. He eventually wrote a book, published in 1912, called *Reminiscences of a Pioneer*, in which he defended the activities of the Prineville vigilantes.

As for Blakely, he was elected to a second term as Crook County sheriff. In 1888 he moved east to Wallowa County where he served as sheriff from 1904 to 1908, then to Baker County, finally ending up in College Place, Washington. He died there on January 23, 1953, at age one hundred, among the last living links with one of the wildest chapters in the history of the American West.

Black Bart

A Famously Friendly Stagecoach Bandit

Before the railroads came in, people and valuables were usually transported throughout the West by stagecoach. Clattering along networks of primitive roads in remote country, they were extremely vulnerable and tempting targets for thieves. Robbers who specialized in stagecoach heists were often referred to as "road agents." A novice highwayman might think the obvious strategy would be to lift the personal valuables from the stage's passengers. The savvy road agent knew the juicy targets were the stages that traveled gold country, usually carrying lots of cash, gold coins, gold dust, and registered mail for the taking. In the mid- and late 1800s southwest Oregon offered plenty of juicy targets.

In 1848 gold was discovered in California and the rush was on. Men, mostly in their twenties and thirties, journeyed to the Golden State not only from places throughout America, but from England, Europe, and other parts of the world as well, hoping to strike it rich. As the horde of gold seekers fanned out across northern California, they made their way into southern Oregon as well, lusting for that glitter of yellow in its streams and rivers.

In 1850 and 1851 the search paid off, with gold strikes on Oregon's Josephine Creek, the Illinois River, and a number of streams in the Jacksonville area. This sparked a second rush of gold seekers from both northern California and Oregon's Willamette Valley, who staked claims along the Rogue, Applegate, and Pistol Rivers, among others. Rowdy mining camps sprang up, and from the prosperity brought by the gold economy, Jacksonville grew into a real community—the first in Jackson County.

By the early 1860s regular stagecoach service had been established between Sacramento and Portland. Run by the California Stage Company, the route was more than seven hundred miles long, and stages ran daily, with one headed south and the other north.

On those stagecoaches, in addition to passengers, rode a variety of items of interest to road agents: cash, gold coins, registered letters filled with gold dust, and other valuables on their way from the goldfields and local businesses to big city banks. A gold shipment carried by stagecoach might commonly be worth as much as ten thousand dollars.

But it wasn't just the fact that southern Oregon was gold country that made the area enticing to stagecoach robbers, but the nature of the country as well and the Siskiyou Mountains in particular.

The wild and remote Siskiyou Mountains straddle the Oregon–California border and lie within Jackson County to the north and Siskiyou County on the south. Their lonely trails seldom saw lawmen, and their rugged terrain worked in favor of outlaws on the run. The Siskiyous were the perfect place to rob a stagecoach.

Road agents figured that out pretty quickly, and several gangs formed during southern Oregon's gold rush days specifically to prey on stagecoaches. Holdups along the Siskiyou Mountains stagecoach roads were a fairly regular occurrence—sometimes as often as one per week.

Planning a stage robbery didn't take a great deal of deep thinking, and the strategy was generally the same. The stage was most vulnerable as it was lumbering uphill with the horses pulling at a slow walk. The road agents would suddenly step from behind a tree or bush, brandishing rifles, shotguns, or pistols, and order the stage driver to halt and throw down the Wells Fargo "express box" that held the loot. Taking an ax to the box, they would remove the goods and vanish into the silent mountains, leaving behind a frustrated driver to continue on his way, his load considerably lightened. But by no means did all road agents get away with the goods.

In May 1857 one of southern Oregon's crack stagecoach drivers, Jack Montgomery—who was always in demand—was hired by the Jacksonville office of the Oregon and California Stage Coach Line to haul a Wells Fargo & Company gold shipment worth about a half million dollars. He was to take it to Portland where Wells Fargo would then arrange to have it shipped to company headquarters in San Francisco. The company offered Montgomery two hundred fifty dollars for the job, and he accepted. Secrecy, for obvious reasons, was paramount, but word of big gold shipments tended to get around.

Pulling a ten-horse stage with the gold stuffed into canvas bags, Montgomery, along with a few passengers and accompanied by two armed guards, made his way north at top speed. But at Umpqua Falls an explosion rocked the trail ahead, sending the horse team into a panicked run that spun the coach out of control.

Montgomery leaped from the stage as rocks crashed down upon it, killing one of the guards. The other guard ran off screaming and then collapsed in the forest. Passengers, trapped in the stage, cried for help as the four bandits who had placed the dynamite charge grabbed as many sacks of gold as they could carry. Montgomery, although injured, tried to stop them but had to run for his life instead, making it to a nearby stage station before falling to the floor unconscious.

Montgomery recovered, but the robbers fared less well. Not long afterward, a group of vigilantes found four men holed up in a cave in the Siskiyou Mountains with several sacks of gold. The posse hanged them on the spot.

Although southern Oregon's gold boom was just about played out by the late 1860s, it didn't cause too much hardship on the part of the road agents since northern California's gold fields were still producing. And that gold still traveled by stage through the Siskiyou Mountains between Oregon and California.

Two of those routes that regularly carried the kinds of cargo coveted by road agents were the Roseburg to Yreka and Roseburg to Redding roads. Sometime in the summer of 1880, Black Bart, who had mainly been working the California side of the Siskiyous, decided that he had not been giving the Oregon side of the mountains the attention it deserved.

Black Bart was fast becoming the most famous and successful stagecoach robber in the West. He had made his debut as a road agent on July 26, 1875, on Funk Hill along the Sonora–Milton stagecoach road in Calaveras County, California. Stagecoach robberies and highwaymen had been a dime a dozen in northern California and southern Oregon since the early 1860s, but in spite of the routine nature of these holdups—if being robbed can be considered a routine experience—Bart had managed to pull off his first heist with a certain flair and presence that had made him an immediate standout.

What stagecoach driver John Shine first noticed about the man standing in the road—besides the shotgun, which unbeknownst to all his victims over the years was always unloaded—was that the road agent said "please" when he ordered the Wells Fargo express box and mail sacks to be thrown to the ground. He wore plain homespun clothes under a duster and a flour sack over his head with eyeholes cut out. The T-shaped slashes he made in the mail sacks to gain entry became another distinctive aspect of his holdup signature.

When the outlaw had finished his work, he had one hundred sixty dollars in gold notes and an undetermined amount of cash and other valuables. The next day, Wells Fargo & Company offered a two hundred fifty dollar reward for the capture of the "flour sack" bandit.

He gave himself his outlaw moniker during his fourth robbery. After relieving the stagecoach driver of about six hundred dollars in gold coins and a check, he left behind a bit of verse:

> *I've labored long for bread*
> *For honor and for riches,*
> *But on my corns too long you've tread*
> *You fine haired sons of bitches*
> *Black Bart, the Po8*

The name Black Bart came from a character in a popular novel of the time and it had caught his fancy. But he was really Charles Boles, in his early forties, with gray hair, a mustache, and neatly trimmed chin whiskers. Standing about five feet eight inches tall, he had a dignified and urbane countenance.

His family immigrated to the United States in the 1830s, settling in Jefferson County, New York. When gold fever struck California, Boles and a cousin headed west, arriving in the goldfields in 1850, hoping to strike it rich. They returned home unsuccessful the following year. He made another ill-fated mining trip to California with his cousin and brother, both of whom died shortly after arriving in San Francisco.

Boles went back to the East, married, had two daughters, and worked and farmed in the Midwest. When the Civil War broke out, he enlisted in the Union Army, mustering in as a private in Company B, 116th Illinois Volunteers on August 13, 1862.

During the war he saw a good deal of action, fighting in such battles as Vicksburg, Arkansas Post, Chickasaw Bayou, Champion Hills, and Black River Ridge. He also marched to Atlanta with General William Tecumseh Sherman. He was wounded in action, rose to the rank of first sergeant, and would likely have been offered an officer's commission if he had not left the army at the end of the war.

After military service he returned home, but over the next decade apparently tired of domestic life and living in the heartland. In the mid-1870s he moved to Montana and then, by 1878, to San Francisco where he posed as prosperous mine owner Charles Bolton, slipping away periodically to ply his real profession. He would never see his wife and daughters again.

By the time he turned a larcenous eye to the Oregon side of the Siskiyou Mountains, he had thirteen stagecoach robberies under his belt, was a favorite subject of newspaper reporters, and was the focus of an all-out investigation by special agents of the Wells Fargo & Company.

Conventional highwayman wisdom said that you robbed a stage coming from the goldfields when presumably there was gold aboard, not when it was going to the fields to pick it up. But Black Bart (his real identity was still unknown) was no conventional road agent, and he made his plans to rob the southbound Roseburg to Yreka stage on September 16, 1880. It was going to be a night job, a tactic that had become something of a specialty with Bart, the cover of darkness making his trademark escapes on foot more effective.

This would be Black Bart's fourteenth stage holdup, and he was becoming more than a nuisance to Wells Fargo & Company. The gold he was stealing belonged to the company or its customers to whom reimbursement for losses company policy

BLACK BART

P 3558

Charles Boles, also known as Black Bart.
Calaveras County Historical Society

demanded. The company was extremely frustrated, even if the robber was a famous folk hero.

Henry Wells and William Fargo had founded Wells Fargo & Company in 1852. Based in San Francisco, the economic center for the northern California gold rush, the company provided banking services, including buying gold and selling bank drafts backed by gold, and delivered gold and other valuables to various points throughout the West. As their success grew, they opened offices in other western cities and even in remote mining camps.

The company's stagecoach empire had its beginning in 1858 when it helped found the Overland Mail Company stage line. Eventually the company took over the western leg of the Pony Express and by 1886 assumed control of virtually all the major stage-line routes in the West, from Nebraska to the Pacific Ocean.

The centerpiece of Wells Fargo & Company's stage operations was the famed Concord Coach. Built in Concord, New Hampshire, and costing about eleven hundred dollars each, they weighed about 2,500 pounds and were each pulled by a team of six horses. Their interiors were leather and damask cloth, and the special "thorough braces" suspension composed of leather strips provided what passed as a comfortable ride for the time period. The company also used another model stage called a Henderson, which was a little lighter than the Concord and could be pulled by four horses.

Sometimes referred to as "mud wagons," they were both designed to carry people and freight through just about any kind of terrain the West could throw at them.

The men who drove the stages or rode shotgun were as tough as they came. Striking out on the trail well before dawn and driving until late at night, they stopped at a stage station along the way to water, feed, and rest the horses—and maybe even get a little food and rest themselves—before hitching up and getting under way again in the early morning darkness. Their job was to get the stage through, no matter what the weather, how deep the mud, or how thick the bandits.

George Chase was just that kind of driver as he guided his horse team up the Oregon side of the road to the 4,466-foot-high

A typical Oregon stagecoach of the late 1800s.
John C. H. Grabill Collection, Library of Congress

Siskiyou Summit. It was sometime between 11:00 p.m. and midnight. Although there was a bright moon out, the carriage lanterns provided a little extra light as they rocked back and forth with every swaying movement of the stage, casting weird and erratic shadows on the road and the trees.

But then, there in the moonlit way, just half a dozen or so miles from the state line, stood a man in work clothes and a linen duster. He had a flour sack over his head and a 12-gauge shotgun pointed at Chase. He politely asked the driver to throw down the express box.

The Wells Fargo & Company express box was what every road agent was after, although none asked for it so graciously as Black Bart. Made by San Francisco cabinetmaker Joseph William Ayer, they were wooden boxes twenty inches long, twelve inches wide, and ten inches high, reinforced with iron straps.

This was where the gold and cash resided. The express boxes were stored in the "boot" of the stage located under the driver's feet. As robberies became more common, the boxes were bolted to the stage to make it more difficult for outlaws to get at them. Eventually, the company went to all-metal boxes.

On this night the wood and iron-strapped express box was chained to the boot at the rear of the stage. Keeping driver Chase covered—he had no shotgun rider with him this run—Bart took an ax and went to work on the box. Next, he went hunting through the mail sacks, slashing them with his trademark T design.

With business completed at just about midnight, he vanished into the mountains, leaving not a trace of evidence for the lawmen who came to investigate the crime scene the following day.

In reporting the incident, the *Yreka* [California] *Journal* noted that the southbound stages were rarely robbed because there was usually not much of value on stages headed in that direction. But the joke was on them, for Black Bart had made off with about one thousand dollars in cash and a purported significant haul in the registered letters. It was, in fact, his most profitable robbery to date.

With a success story like that, how could anyone resist coming back for a replay? Certainly not Black Bart. A week later, on Thursday, September 23, he was back in Jackson County. This time he was after the northbound Yreka to Roseburg stage.

Just a few miles north of the state line, the driver (who was either George Chase or Nort Eddings) heard the familiar road agent cry of "throw down the box." There was Black Bart with his duster, flour-sack face, and unloaded shotgun. The box landed on the packed dirt with a thud. Bart fell upon it immediately, fleeing a few minutes later, a thousand dollars richer. As usual, he left no incriminating evidence behind.

Back in town, the *Jacksonville Democratic Times,* in noting that the driver had been previously robbed by a road agent at the exact same location, quoted the driver as saying that he was "getting tired of this sport."

On September 26, President Rutherford Hayes, the first US president to visit the West Coast, accompanied by General Sherman, traveled on a stage from California to Oregon taking the Siskiyou Pass road. If Black Bart had waited a few more days to pull off robbery number fifteen, he might have really made history.

Black Bart moved back down into California after that, but continued to rob the Roseburg stage line. He finally made his fatal error on Funk Hill on November 3, 1883, the site of his very first depredation. In fleeing the scene of the holdup under a hail of bullets, he left behind a handkerchief with a laundry mark. James Hume, chief of Wells Fargo & Company detectives, and his agents, who had been chasing Bart for eight years, found his San Francisco launderer, who identified Black Bart as upstanding citizen Charles Bolton, who was really Charles Boles.

Before long they had Boles in custody and had convinced him to plead guilty to the Funk Hill robbery rather than risk a trial for the twenty-eight or twenty-nine other stagecoach holdups he was suspected of committing. Never admitting to any other robberies but the one, he was sentenced to six years in San Quentin prison. He was released in just over four, in January 1888, for good behavior.

Black Bart promptly disappeared, although rumors of him robbing stages from Colorado to Alaska popped up for years. One persistent story told of a dignified, graying gentleman who was shot to death while trying to rob a stagecoach in Nevada and buried in a shallow grave amongst the sagebrush. But there were never any verified sightings of the old road agent after he left prison. If the ghost of Charles Boles, aka Black Bart, roams the earth, he must surely be somewhere waiting along the dark and fading stagecoach trails of the Siskiyou Mountains.

Range Wars

Sheep Men Versus Cattle Ranchers

Even for men used to seeing slaughter, this was an appalling sight. Five hundred sheep, belonging to Fred Smith of Paulina, lay dead in the desert near Grindstone. Shot to death, the corpses lay scattered amongst the lava rocks and clumps of sagebrush. Above this grisly scene, the arch of cobalt blue, crystal-clear, high desert sky stretched from horizon to horizon. It was New Year's Day 1905, and it was war.

That afternoon, six men on horseback, disguised with masks and blackface, had descended upon the hapless shepherd as he had tended his flock. Surrounding the frightened and unarmed man, the riders leapt from their mounts and dragged him to the ground, holding him immobile as they tied his wrists and ankles and blindfolded his eyes. Now, with the shepherd incapacitated, his sheep were helpless too. The riders remounted their horses and began rounding the animals up, gathering together the herd of about seven hundred. With loud cries and war whoops, they drove them a short distance away from where the shepherd lay, and opened fire with rifles, dropping about five hundred sheep on the spot. The survivors ran off into the desert in a panic, destined to be dinner for predators. Their awful task complete, the six riders galloped off. It was not the first such slaughter this lonely country had seen in recent years, and it would not be the last.

During the mid- and late 1800s, cattle ranching was king on Oregon's rolling rangelands and high plains country east of the

Cascade Mountains. Stockmen from the Willamette Valley in western Oregon had been bringing their cattle to these parts each spring and summer since the 1860s to take advantage of the lush and nutritious range grass. They also drove their herds of cattle—as many as one hundred thousand head—through the region on their way to help feed gold miners in the rugged mountains of northeast Oregon. During this period, cattle empires, such as the Teal & Coleman Ranch on Trout Creek at Willowdale, were being formed throughout the region, along with countless smaller operations. These cattle barons, great and small, looked upon their empire and saw that it was good—until the sheep men came.

By the 1880s cattlemen and sheep men were sharing the range, and not always amicably. During this period and over following decades, railroad tracks were being laid from the main line along the Columbia River into central Oregon. The town of Shaniko, on the empty plains of Wasco County, was established in 1879 on the route of the Columbia Southern rail line. By 1903 Shaniko was being called the Wool Capital of the World and was the primary distribution center for virtually all the sheep and wool produced across central and eastern Oregon. The railroad provided a more efficient and economical means for cattlemen and sheep men to bring their goods to world markets, encouraging production but also competition for the unregulated open range.

From a stockman's point of view, his cattle were here first and the open range was his. The shepherd and his sheep were interlopers, taking what wasn't theirs. There was a lot about sheep and shepherds the cattlemen didn't like. First, there were just too many sheep. It's estimated that there were about 130,000 sheep grazing in Wasco County between 1885 and 1910. By the early 1900s, perhaps as many as 50,000 cattle and 340,000 sheep shared Crook County's Ochoco and Maury Mountains. Any way a cattleman looked at it, he was outnumbered.

Something else that rankled the rancher was a sheep's eating habits. Cattle ate bunchgrass and other wild, native grasses. Sheep ate those too, but they also grazed on forbs and virtually every other weed and flower out on the range, snipping them off close to the ground. Cattlemen could tell when a herd of sheep had moved through an area because it was stripped of nearly all of its vegetation, leaving a virtual moonscape behind. That didn't sit well with the stockmen.

And finally, it was the very nature of the sheep business that rubbed cattlemen the wrong way. The shepherd usually tended his charges on foot. In cowboy country, men rode horses. For that, the ranchers looked down upon the shepherd and regarded him as an inferior being.

It was just plain getting harder and harder to be a cattleman. The ranchers let their cattle graze year round on the open range. In the spring, they moved their herds into the high country of the Blue Mountains and eastern slopes of the Cascade Mountains where the animals could dine on the nutritious new grass growth. But as more cattle, horses, and sheep came to be grazed in the region, conflicts erupted. The cattlemen raced to get their cows into the mountains first while the sheep men drove their flocks from Morrow, Gilliam, Wasco, Umatilla, Sherman, and Crook Counties with the same idea in mind. At the same time, stockmen from western Oregon were driving increasing numbers of their livestock to graze the Crooked River country, making the situation all the worse. The local cattlemen seethed with resentment. It was only a matter of time before something had to give.

The ranchers out in the Izee and Bear Valley country of Grant County got fed up first. They complained that the sheep men bringing their flocks to the Snow Mountain and Izee country were letting them graze right down to the fenced boundaries of the ranchers' pastures, eating "out their door yards." That was too much. Something needed to be done.

So stockmen of the Izee country had a little meeting one day in 1896 and formed a civic organization they called the Izee Sheep Shooters. Their new organization would discourage the sheep men through the persuasive methods of such famous western diplomats as Colt, Winchester, and Smith & Wesson.

Whenever a flock of sheep came too close to a cattleman's ranch, the Izee Sheep Shooters would ride out to explain to the shepherd the error of his ways. They would hold him and his camp tender at gunpoint while they shot as many of the offending sheep as possible. It wasn't long before word got out among cattlemen about what a fine job the Izee Sheep Shooters were doing, removing those hoofed locusts from Grant County.

It just so happened that the ranchers to the west in Paulina were having the same problem, with sheep men from Wasco County and the lower John Day River area bringing their sheep onto Crook County rangeland and crowding the Paulina ranchers' cattle. The Paulina ranchers invited a representative from the Izee Sheep Shooters to come talk to them about forming a similar organization of their own. Out of neighborly civic duty, Izee cattleman Henry Snodgrass volunteered to speak to the group.

The meeting was held in late July 1898 under a ponderosa pine tree somewhere along Wolf Creek in Crook County. An hour before midnight, nearly forty men gathered around a roaring campfire, listening to Snodgrass describe how the Izee Sheep Shooters operated and what its mission was. Secrecy and, above all, loyalty were imperative to success and for evading the law.

The leader of the Izee Sheep Shooters, his weathered face alternating between light and shadow as the flames of the bonfire shot embers toward the black sky, leaned forward and declared that if any man did not want to join the brotherhood of sheep haters and was unwilling to do what was necessary to drive the sheep out of the country, he should leave now and go home to bed.

The rules of the game were so serious that an oath had to be taken by each man who wished to be a member. If while they were engaged in killing sheep it became necessary to kill a shepherd or camp tender, the victim would be buried on the spot. If one of their members were killed in the course of a sheep-shooting operation, his body would be brought home for burial with no word made of the cause or circumstances of his demise. And if any of their company were apprehended by the law and made to stand trial, his fellow vigilantes were obligated to lie under oath to protect him.

Snodgrass went around the campfire, man by man, and made each swear to the conditions he had just set forth. For three of the attending ranchers, it was too much to ask. Fred Powell, Billie Congleton, and Sam Courtney got up and rode off home to bed. The others stayed behind and the Inland Sheep Shooters were born. Other sheep shooters sprang up locally, here and there, on the Oregon rangelands. This vigilante movement spread from Bear Valley to Paulina in 1898, to Camp Creek in 1902, and to Silver Lake in 1903. Many of these were rather loose and informal affairs with a few ranchers occasionally saddling up to "touch up" a herd of sheep, as one stockman put it. But the Inland Sheep Shooters would become the largest and most effective of the bunch. Between 1898 and 1906 the Paulina ranchers who had sworn a blood oath that dark night by the bonfire would destroy thousands of sheep and murder one man.

The first thing the Paulina stockmen did was to establish a boundary, which they called a "deadline," over which they would let no sheep pass. That deadline started on the summit of Wolf Mountain across and over Paulina Butte, then down the Crooked River to the Paulina ranches. They marked this boundary with blazed trees and sent a warning to the sheep men that any sheep that crossed south of that line would be killed. A shepherd caught in the forbidden zone would risk the same fate.

By the time the nineteenth century had turned into the twentieth, the Inland Sheep Shooters had become bolder, progressing well beyond "touching up" a few flocks of sheep here and there. The biggest sheep slaughter the Paulina stockmen ever pulled off was at Benjamin Lake near the Crook-Lake County line on April 28, 1903. That spring, three different sheep men from Summer Lake had brought their sheep to Benjamin Lake, making for a combined flock of about 2,700. The sheep men and the camp tenders were armed and had let word go around that they didn't hold much truck with the cattlemen's threats to stay out of "their territory."

But the Inland Sheep Shooters would tolerate no defiance of their orders. Arriving at camp and wearing masks, a posse of sheep shooters jumped the herder on duty, put a sack over his head, and left one of their own to guard him. Then they went looking for the tender, whom they found about a mile away. Slipping a sack over his head, too, they returned him to camp and placed him under guard as well. The sheep shooters swung back on their mounts and casually rode out of camp and into the immense flock of sheep. Calmly, and with grim calculation, they began firing. When they were done, their rifle barrels red-hot and the smoke from their rounds filling the air (along with the bleatings of stricken sheep), only 300 of the original 2,700 animals remained alive.

The sheep killings continued. In February 1904 five masked and armed men attacked a camp containing three thousand head of sheep near Silver Lake. They shot and clubbed the animals, destroying a substantial number before escaping into the desert. Four months later, ten masked men killed more than two thousand sheep owned by sheep men Grube and Parker forty miles south of Silver Lake. More than a thousand sheep died in a raid on Little Summit Prairie in the Ochoco Mountains in July of the same year. The toll on the sheep and sheep men was mounting.

While direct defiance by sheep men of the sheep shooters' directive to stay north of their deadline brought deadly retribution, even minor transgressions were dealt with swiftly and decisively. If a shepherd tried sneaking over the line to let his flock feed a little on the cow side of the deadline and then slipped back to the sheep side, the sheep shooters crossed over to pay him a visit. One story tells of a big, red-bearded sheep man from Tennessee who liked to make regular quick trips south of the deadline to let his sheep graze, and then ease the flock back north. With a .45 caliber Colt revolver and .45-60 Winchester rifle at his side, he laughed at any suggestion that the cattlemen could cause him trouble.

But one afternoon, while taking a nap on "his side" of the deadline, he awoke to the sight of a Smith & Wesson revolver stuffed against his face. Then came a crack of thunder as a slug took a piece of skin off his nose and nearly shot out one of his eyes. The masked men took his boots and guns and disappeared. When the shepherd hobbled barefooted into his camp an hour later, he found a note signed by the Inland Sheep Shooters telling him where he could find his boots and gun and advising him that he was now shy five hundred sheep. When the Tennessean rushed to check his flock, he found he was missing 550.

A herd of sheep in Crook County, tended by a shepherd and his dog.
Bowman Museum and Crook County Historical Society

The sheep shooters didn't just limit their works to fighting sheep men and their flocks. They also killed Indians when the opportunity presented itself. Although it had been nearly forty years since the Paiute Indian wars had ended in the region, there were plenty of ranchers who were old enough to remember those days of terror and did not look kindly upon the remaining Native Americans.

In one well-known incident, rancher John Hyde of Izee was riding through Bear Valley in Grant County in October 1898 when he happened upon a band of Indians camped along Deer Creek. The Indians accused the rancher of stealing some horses and tried to work their way behind him. Hyde managed to break away and galloped home to mobilize the Izee Sheep Shooters.

The next morning a heavily armed committee of sheep shooters was hot on the Indians' trail. The sheep shooters caught up with them a ways downstream. Shooting broke out almost immediately. The headman, Chief Albert, died when fourteen slugs slammed into his body. Sheep shooter George Cutting fell dead from Indian fire. The Indians broke and ran, but the sheep shooters caught up to them, dispatching the Indian who killed Cutting. They shot a few of the Indians' ponies for good measure, and then reined their own toward home, fully satisfied with the morning's work.

The local newspaper, the *Prineville Review*, as well as newspapers throughout the state, had been writing a stream of editorials condemning the sheep killings and the perpetrators. On December 29, 1904, the "Corresponding Secretary of Crook County's Sheep-Shooting Association of Eastern Oregon" actually wrote a letter to the *Morning Oregonian* in Portland providing an annual report of eight thousand to ten thousand sheep slaughtered during the last "shooting season." He also suggested that the governor and state government butt out of their business. The letter sparked statewide outrage among decent citizens.

The sheep men had tried to work out their differences with the stockmen. In late June 1904 the Central Oregon Wool Growers Association held a meeting in Antelope to discuss the range war that was clearly getting out of hand, noting that sheep killings had begun earlier than usual that year. The association offered a fifteen hundred dollar reward for information about the sheep shooters and appointed several emissaries to meet with the cattlemen to discuss a truce. But it was no go. The sheep killings continued, and the sheep men's sheds and haystacks were burned on a regular basis.

Perhaps the most horrific crime against the sheep men and their sheep happened in April 1904. A shepherd who had recently emigrated from Ireland to find himself overseeing a herd of sheep near Fort Rock was paid a visit by a group of masked men one day. They warned him to remove his flock from the area. He paid them no heed. A couple of weeks later they returned, riding into the flock of more than two thousand sheep. Their shouting and yelling panicked the animals and they began to run, stampeding blindly before the masked horsemen. They had no clue they were being herded toward a nearby cliff until they began plunging over the edge in waves.

It was not as if there wasn't any law in these parts. But for the few sheriffs and their deputies who patrolled this country, the task of catching a sheep shooter was formidable. The vigilantes usually traveled at night and were heavily armed. Any lawman who rode off into the mountains in the dark to pursue these outlaws would probably not come back. Although the Inland Sheep Shooters were made up of local ranchers, only they knew the identities of their members, and they would never tell.

But when prominent Prineville merchant J. C. Conn disappeared one day, the law had to do something. Conn, who was a known opponent of the sheep shooters, had grabbed his rifle on the morning of March 4, 1904, and headed out into the wilderness to do some hunting. He was never seen alive again.

When he didn't return home as scheduled, his friends became concerned and launched a search that finally yielded Conn's body about a mile west of Silver Lake on April 21. A revolver with one

A flock of sheep killed by Izee Sheep Shooters.
Bowman Museum and Crook County Historical Society

Sheep camp on McKay Creek.
Bowman Museum and Crook County Historical Society

discharged shell lay alongside. At first, it appeared to be a suicide, but further investigation showed it to be murder. It appeared that his killers had searched Conn's body for what was believed to be evidence identifying members of the Inland Sheep Shooters and their crimes. An arrest was made, but no one was ever convicted.

Ironically, the range war that probably killed at least ten thousand sheep and one man was ended not by lawmen but by the stroke of the pen. In 1902 the federal government withdrew much of the public lands in the Blue Mountains from public domain, establishing the Blue Mountains Forest Reserve, which would eventually become a national forest. In the fall of 1906, the federal government divided those lands into grazing allotments for both cattlemen and sheep men, guaranteeing them places to graze their herds. Since they no longer were in direct competition for grazing grounds, the threat the two groups once posed to each other vanished, and the range war ended.

No one was ever prosecuted for the years of sheep killing, property destruction, and murder. True to the blood oath those thirty-five or so stockmen took around the bonfire that late July night in 1898, the members of the Inland Sheep Shooters took the knowledge of their comrades' identities with them to the grave.

Bill Miner

The Grey Fox

Bill Miner must have been tempted to pull the gray hairs out of his head as he and partner Guy Harshman watched, dumbfounded, as the train they intended to rob this dark night clattered on by them. It was supposed to have stopped long enough for the two, along with a third accomplice hiding nearby, to climb aboard and relieve it of valuables. By the time the three would-be train robbers had realized their mistake, their prey was disappearing down the tracks and into the darkness.

It was Miner's first try at robbing a train, and career changes are always difficult—especially for aging outlaws. He would eventually become a pretty successful train robber in other places, but Oregon is where he got his start, albeit a rocky start.

Bill Miner was a career criminal almost from the beginning. Born Ezra Allen Miner, near Onondaga, Michigan, in 1847, he eventually began going by Bill. His father died suddenly in the mid-1850s. Due to financial difficulties his mother was forced to sell off the family property to pay debts and moved her brood to a mining town in Placer County, California, around 1860.

In his teens now, it was here in the rough-and-tumble California gold camps that young Bill Miner began getting into trouble. At eighteen he made his crime debut by stealing several hundred dollars from the mining company he was working for, lucking out when his employer declined to prosecute him.

He joined the Union Army in April 1864 and was assigned to a military base in Sacramento. Not much for authority, he deserted four months later. A life of crime looked better to Bill Miner than the discipline of military service or, for that matter, the day-to-day drudgery of the law-abiding citizen.

Crude holdups of unsuspecting pedestrians in dark alleys and horse thievery were Miner's early specialties. He earned his first prison sentence of three years in San Quentin in 1866 for stealing eight bucks—with assistance from one of many accomplices he would have over the years—from a ranch hand.

Once out of prison, he immediately resumed his nefarious activities, adding the lucrative business of stagecoach robbery to his repertoire of crime. For a time he expanded his criminal activities to Colorado before returning to his adopted home state of California.

Over the years Miner became an increasingly famous bandit, noted for his persuasive smooth talk and gentlemanly and courteous demeanor. In his later years he became known as the Grey Fox. When he was plying his trade, Miner would say that he was "on the rob." He is sometimes given credit for inventing the holdup man's quintessential phrase, "hands up," but there is no proof of this and it's likely not true.

If Miner and his endless parade of partners in crime over the years were good at thievery, Miner was also good at something else—getting caught. Whenever he did a crime, apprehension and prison were virtually certain. Bill spent a lot of time on the inside of San Quentin State Prison, looking out.

On June 17, 1901, Miner was sprung from San Quentin after serving nearly twenty years for stagecoach robbery. He was fifty-four years old and had spent almost thirty-four of those years behind bars. No longer having family in California (his mother had died while he was in prison and his brother had died in the army), Miner went north to Washington State where his two sisters lived.

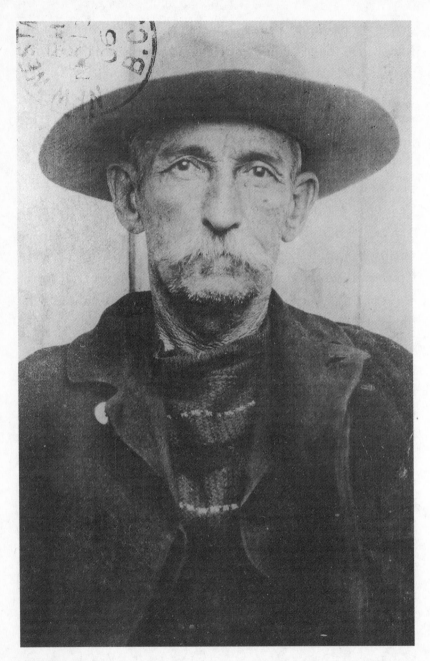

Bill Miner.

Glenbow Archive NA-837-1

Miner settled into honest work at an oyster bed operation in Samish Bay, just south of Bellingham. Using one of his standard aliases, William Morgan, he was gray-haired and personable. His coworkers had no clue about his real background.

After a couple of years, the life of a law-abiding citizen was beginning to give him an itch. The opportunity came to scratch when he received a communiqué from an old San Quentin con buddy who was released a year after Miner. His name was Z. G. Harshman, variously referred to as Gay, Guy, and Gary.

Harshman was working down in Oregon at the Farr Brothers Lumber Company along the Columbia River outside of the town of Goble, about thirty-five miles north of Portland. He had been thinking about robbing a train and wondered if his old friend Bill wanted in.

Miner took a trip to Goble to talk the plan over with Harshman, and it sounded to him like a good idea. Besides, this honest citizen stuff just wasn't working out and Miner was looking to get back into his old trade. The trouble was that when Miner went back into San Quentin for his last prison term, it was 1881 and the Wild West was still wild. In the years he had been in the big house, things had changed quite a bit. There were new technologies and the West was far tamer than the place he had left.

Most important, at least from Miner's perspective, was the way stagecoaches had been replaced by trains. Miner was just going to have to adapt to the times and learn the art of train robbery.

Stagecoaches had always been very vulnerable to holdups. They moved slowly on bad roads and trails, usually far from civilization where lawmen were few and far between. Because travel was by horse, stage, and wagon, by the time a posse reached the site of the crime, the perpetrators were usually long gone.

Z. G. Harshman.
Oregon State Archives

As more railroad lines were built, connecting more communities, trains had become the standard for traveling long distances throughout the West. As romantic as stagecoaches might have seemed, few people of the day missed them. They were extremely uncomfortable vehicles—slow, bumpy, and dusty—and always at risk from highwaymen.

Even though trains were a far more secure way to transport gold and cash, they were not invulnerable; and although train robbery was not nearly as common as stage robberies used to be, every now and then some crooks took a crack at it.

One of the more famous Oregon train robberies was the July 1, 1895, waylaying of a Southern Pacific Railroad train in Cow Creek Canyon, Douglas County. Forcing the train to stop by setting off dynamite as it passed, the bandits intimidated the man in the express car into opening the door. After raiding the express car of its loot, they went through the passenger compartments, relieving the hapless travelers of their valuables as well. Two of the three robbers—Jim Poole and John Case—were eventually caught and sentenced to prison, but the money they stole was never found. It was obviously possible for men on foot to successfully rob a train, although getting away with it might be a different story.

At the beginning of a new century, Bill Miner, although considerably grayer and older now, was sure that with just a little retraining and practice he could meet this new professional challenge. But they needed another man to pull off the job.

Miner went back to Samish Bay and recruited seventeen-year-old Charles Hoehn, with whom he had struck up a friendship while living in the area. Hoehn had been in a little trouble with the law for petty theft and had spent some time in jail. He also apparently admired Miner, making it relatively easy for Miner to recruit Hoehn into their new gang. In late August 1903 Miner and Hoehn went south to rendezvous with Harshman in Goble.

The three men worked together at the lumber company for a short time while they refined their plans. Their target would be the express car of an Oregon Railway and Navigation Company train that traveled the tracks along the Columbia River. The date they picked for the robbery was September 19. The location decided upon was Clarnie, an Oregon Railway and Navigation Company station about fifteen miles east of Portland. The time of the robbery would be the dark of night.

The three men arrived at the appointed place, staking out a railroad stop signal where the train would halt when the red light flashed on. Miner and Harshman scrambled up the bank to shoot down on the train while Hoehn hunkered down by the signal.

Charles Hoehn.
Oregon State Archives

Now they waited for their prize to come by. Eventually, in the distance, they could hear the train approaching. They braced themselves for the assault. But something wasn't right. With no previous railroading experience among them, none of outlaws noticed that the stop signal was on a different track than the one on which their train was traveling. The engineer didn't stop because the stop signal was not for him, and he drove his train on by, oblivious to Miner, Harshman, and Hoehn watching from the sidelines in frustration. If the three intended to become successful train robbers, they definitely needed more practice.

They may have been discouraged, but not enough to keep them from trying again. Back in Goble the three men continued to work at the Farr Brothers Lumber Company for cover and as a temporary source of income while they pondered another train heist. This time a bit more thought and planning would go into it, including a better escape strategy. The escape plan for the first robbery was simply to hightail it to Portland and get lost in the crowd. And they needed to do more advance scouting, too.

Once again they would target the Oregon Railway and Navigation Company, the Fast Express Number 6 that departed from Portland at 8:15 p.m. on September 23, 1903, bound for Chicago.

A few days earlier, Hoehn had procured a small rowboat, which he rowed down the Columbia River to the town of Corbett, some fifteen miles east of Portland, and stashed it along the banks. He then hitched a train ride back to Goble.

This time their plan was more elaborate. Miner and Harshman would sneak on board the train when it stopped at the Troutdale Station. Hoehn would walk about three miles up the tracks, near where he had hidden the getaway boat on the river, and wait for the train to arrive. Miner and Harshman would force the engineer to stop the train, the gang would blow open the express car door, which was where cash, gold, and other treasure would be, and then escape by rowboat back to Goble. No one would ever be the wiser.

At about 9:00 p.m. the train rolled into the Troutdale Station. Miner and Harshman had black masks tied over their faces to conceal their identities and carried pistols and a couple of sticks of dynamite. As the train came to a stop, the two bandits quietly stole on board the baggage car just behind engine tender.

As the train chugged away from the station, the two made their way onto the engine tender and surprised engineer Ollie Barrett and fireman H. F. Stevenson, pulling their pistols and ordering the train to stop at milepost 21 where Hoehn lay in wait. They promised them "death would be their only reward if there was any trickery." Barrett complied as Hoehn, gripping his rifle, emerged from trackside to meet his compatriots.

Once the train had stopped, the two trainmen were hustled out of the cab and ordered to escort the bandits to the express car. As they stood before the locked doors, the outlaws' goal now was to get inside as quickly, efficiently, and, preferably, as quietly as possible.

At first, they tried to do it the easy way, demanding that engineer Barrett tell the express car messenger to open up. Barrett did as he was told, calling to messenger Fred Korner that it was he, Barrett, and to open up.

When the train first came to a stop, Korner and his assistant, Solomon Glick, thought the train might be having engine trouble or some other problem. But as soon as they heard Barrett's request, the two knew larceny was afoot. Korner made no response to Barrett. Glick put out the lights inside the car.

Disappointed with the result of that approach, the three outlaws confabbed for a few minutes, deciding what to do. The answer soon became obvious. The men inside wouldn't open the door to the express car and Miner, Harshman, and Hoehn wanted what was inside. That's why they'd brought the dynamite.

Attaching a couple of dynamite sticks to long poles that they then leaned against the express car door, they lit the fuses and took cover. The explosion did its job, opening a hole in the door more than large enough to gain them entry. The bandits moved toward the gaping hole, peering into the express car in anticipation of the riches it held.

Accounts vary as to whether the sudden blast that came next was directed from the back door of the car or through the shattered door, but express messenger Korner had a shotgun on board and used it as Harshman, Miner, and Hoehn approached. Harshman was first in line and took pellets to the head and chest, wounding him severely. They dropped him on

Train station, Hood River County, early 1900s.
Hood River County Historical Museum

the spot. Engineer Barrett was accidentally hit in the shoulder, but was not seriously harmed.

This wasn't part of the plan, and the two bandits left standing had to think fast. By now, the passengers and other crewmen had figured out that a robbery was in progress. The conductor was busy calming the passengers. Later newspaper reports said that the conductor counseled his passengers to secure their valuables in case the robbers came through the passenger cars. This sent the travelers into a panic as they began to hide their wallets, watches, and jewelry in nooks and crannies throughout the train.

Out in the dark Charles Hoehn had thought the fastest. At the sound of Korner's shotgun, he ran for the rowboat, hidden nearby, and was gone. Now the Grey Fox was on his own, left with a wounded partner and outnumbered by the train crew. Assessing the situation, he ran too, following Hoehn into the darkness to the boat. Harshman lay in the ditch by the tracks, barely conscious, bleeding and groaning.

Returning to the station, the crew reported the robbery to the Multnomah County Sheriff's Department in Portland and the local Pinkerton office. County Sheriff William Storey and the Pinkerton Portland Superintendent Captain James Nevins made their way by train to the robbery site accompanied by a group of law enforcement officers. Arriving after midnight, they found the wounded Harshman along the tracks and took him into custody, transporting the failed train robber to Portland's Good Samaritan Hospital, where he was not expected to live.

Meanwhile, Miner and Hoehn had regrouped at the boat and launched it into the Columbia River, making their way in the darkness to the Washington side. When Hoehn asked about Harshman, Miner lied and said that he was dead. They floated and rowed downstream, eventually putting ashore near Kalama, Washington, and going their separate ways.

As daylight broke on September 24, search parties were combing both the Oregon and Washington sides of the Columbia River for the two desperadoes. No trace of either could be found. Although it was not one of Miner's more remunerative ventures, it would be one of the few crimes for which he was never caught.

In the hospital Harshman surprised everyone by recovering, although he was not being at all cooperative with the police. He gave them a fake name, Jim Conners, and said that four other robbers were involved in the crime. He gave fake names for his accomplices, real and imaginary, as well.

About a week later, investigators got a break and figured out Harshman's real identity and his specialty, counterfeiting, for which he had served time in California and Washington. With the jig up, Harshman became more cooperative and fingered Miner and Hoehn.

Accounts differ on exactly where he was arrested, but Charles Hoehn was picked up by law officers in Washington State in early October and remanded to the Multnomah County Sheriff's Department.

Charged with train robbery and assault with a deadly weapon, Hoehn was sentenced to ten years at the Oregon State Penitentiary in Salem. Harshman got twelve.

Up north, the Grey Fox was on the run once again. Some reports say he stopped for a while to visit one of his sisters, Mary Jane Wellman, leaving behind an overcoat caked with the blood of his former friend, Z. G. Harshman. Other accounts report that when he stepped off the rowboat on the Washington State side of the Columbia River on September 23, 1903, he turned north and kept on going.

Either way, he eventually ended up in British Columbia and hooked up with his old San Quentin cellmate Jake Terry. Terry reportedly once worked as a railroad engineer and knew something about railroads and railroading. When the two teamed up, they got a good thing going that included introducing Canada to its first train robbery on September 10, 1904, forty miles east of Vancouver.

But Miner's penchant for getting caught haunted him again, and Canadian authorities captured him after an unsuccessful train robbery in 1906. He was sentenced to life in prison at the British Columbia Penitentiary in New Westminster.

He escaped on August 8, 1907, under suspicious circumstances. It is now believed that that the British Columbia government allowed him to break out in return for retrieving and giving back three hundred thousand dollars in securities that he and

Terry (who was dead by now, killed in a fight with his ex-wife's husband) had stolen during the 1904 robbery. Instead, he left Canada for good.

The Grey Fox ended his career in Georgia, where he robbed a train in 1911 at age sixty-four. Captured, as usual, he was sentenced to twenty years on a convict road gang. Because of his age and poor health, he was transferred to a prison farm in Midgeville. Too sick to work on a road gang, he wasn't too ill to escape, which he did twice—in 1911 and 1912. He was quickly captured each time. Returned to the prison farm for the second time, he died on September 12, 1913, at age sixty-six.

Harry Tracy and Dave Merrill

The False Face Bandits

Marion County Sheriff Frank W. Durbin, exhausted from the chase, finally had to admit that the two dangerous and violent fugitives had gotten away. By now they were probably across the Columbia River and well into Washington State. When they had escaped from the Oregon State Penitentiary a week earlier, law enforcement officials had been more than confident that they would apprehend the outlaws quickly. But despite a manhunt involving hundreds of searchers, the Oregon National Guard, and bloodhounds and a handler brought in from out of state, the criminals had simply vanished. Posses had even surrounded the pair a time or two. Not only did the pair get away, they had even set a trap for their pursuers.

The entire affair had been a media circus. Reporters were following the searchers everywhere, and some posse members had spent more time posing for news photographers' cameras and giving interviews to reporters than looking for the escapees. Millions of people across the country were reading about the search every day in the papers, and worse, from a lawman's point of view, they were turning these two criminals into folk heroes. The newspapers were comparing them, favorably, to Frank and Jesse James, the Daltons and the Youngers, and other infamous outlaws from the old-time West.

Spurred on by all the publicity, hordes of gawkers followed the posse by motor car, horseback, and on foot, hoping to be there when the capture was made. They only got in the way instead.

The newspapers had been right about one thing, anyway. When news of the prison breakout hit the streets, the *Portland Oregonian* predicted that escaped convicts Harry Tracy and Dave Merrill would not be taken easily. That prediction was turning out to be all too true.

On June 9, 1902, Harry Tracy and Dave Merrill were into the third year of their prison terms for a string of armed robberies and assaults in the Portland area. Tracy, in his mid-twenties, was serving a twenty-year sentence, while his partner in crime, Merrill, who was a few years older, got off with a lighter sentence of thirteen years. The details of their violent escape that day are well recorded. But who on the outside helped them will likely forever remain a mystery.

The Oregon State Penitentiary is situated in farm country on the eastern outskirts of Oregon's capital city, Salem. In the early 1900s, the State Street electric trolley car line terminated at the prison, which was made up of a complex of brick buildings and an open exercise yard.

Surrounding the prison compound were two hundred acres of state-owned land that the inmates farmed as part of their work program. Inside the compound was the foundry building where most of the inmates worked. In addition, prisoners also occupied themselves with tailoring, shoemaking, carpentry, and other trades.

Work was an important part of an inmate's daily routine as a way to keep him occupied, disciplined, and productive. In fact, the state made a pretty good bit of change from the labors of the inmates. Between 1905 and 1907, for example, the convicts brought a little more than $38,000 into state coffers between crops grown on the prison farm, products made in the foundry, and the value of convict labor provided for roadwork.

During this time period the penitentiary typically housed between three hundred and four hundred inmates and retained thirty or forty guards and other prison staff. In 1907 inmates entering the prison to begin serving their sentences were given close-cropped haircuts and issued gray prison uniforms. The gray uniforms were a relatively recent reform. Previously, all prisoners wore the striped prison outfits that later were employed as a disciplinary measure.

When Tracy and Merrill served their time at the Oregon State pen, striped suits were the fashion for all the cons. Both men had a bad reputation among the guards as uncooperative troublemakers who were prone to violence. It didn't take distinctive prison garb to remind the guards that these two needed to be watched closely and treated with caution.

Indeed, Tracy had already caused law officers more than a little trouble shortly after his arrest. Tracy's wife, Mollie (who was Dave Merrill's sister), managed to smuggle a pistol to her husband while he was lodged in jail awaiting trial. As he was being taken to court in March 1899, he broke away from his captors, only to surrender a short time later after a brief shootout with police.

On that June 9 morning, Tracy, Merrill, and a procession of 160 or so of their fellow prisoners shuffled into the foundry building to begin the day's work. At a predetermined spot the two men suddenly bent low and ducked beneath a workbench. When they stood up, they were in the possession of two Winchester rifles. The shocked and unarmed guards ran for safety. Tracy raised his rifle, aimed at guard F. B. Ferrell as he fled, and shot him in the back, killing him instantly.

$1500.00 for each one who escaped from the Oregon State Penitentiary on the morning of June 9, 1902.

HARRY TRACY   DAVID MERRILL

Harry Tracy and Dave Merrill.
Oregon State Archives

Now the two outlaws ran for the foundry door, bound for the prison yard. One inmate, Frank Inghram, tried to stop the escapees and was shot in the leg for his trouble.

Bursting out into the prison yard, Tracy and Merrill began firing at the guards posted on the prison's southwest and northwest walls. The guards ducked for cover and then returned fire. Both men were known to be expert shots with rifle and pistol, and all the guards knew it. If there were any doubters among the bunch, Tracy was about to make them believers. Bracing his rifle securely against his shoulder, Tracy took careful aim at a guard on the north wall 150 yards away and coolly squeezed the trigger. A man known to history as S. Jones fell back dead.

The prison yard was now like a minor battle scene. Bullets whizzed between the escaping prisoners and their keepers, taking chunks out of the prison walls and kicking up dust as they hit the ground. Prisoners were in a panic, dashing from the line of fire while guards worked to keep them under control, hoping to prevent a riot or mass breakout attempt from developing.

Under cover of this confusion and mayhem, Tracy and Merrill found a ladder. Laying it quickly against the prison wall, they scrambled up it and then dropped down on the other side of the wall. They began running along the wall, heading east. Freedom was near. Suddenly, they bumped into two more guards, named Tiffany and Ross, and took them hostage.

Stories differ on exactly what happened next. Some reports say that a guard on the wall above saw the two escapees with their hostages and began firing down on them. Another story says that the hostages ran. Either way, guard B. F. Tiffany ended up dead, shot by Tracy. Ross dropped to the ground and lay still. At this point, more intent on escape than killing, Tracy and Merrill left Ross breathing and ran across the open farm ground and melted into the surrounding woods.

Dave Merrill was a small-time thief and thug who hailed from Vancouver, Washington. Exactly how he and Tracy became partners is not known for certain. One story, probably myth, says that they met in a Portland saloon when Tracy saved Merrill from a logger who had accused Merrill of cheating at cards and was about to give him a good thumping. Tracy, supposedly, stepped up and knocked the logger unconscious. After that, the two outlaws became fast friends.

Of Tracy, a little more is known. He was born Harry Severns about 1877 in Wisconsin. Sometime in the early 1890s he went west, ending up in Colorado and Utah, where he was involved in a variety of criminal pursuits, mostly burglary and cattle rustling.

In 1897 he was arrested for burglary in Utah and sentenced to a prison term at the Utah State Penitentiary. Assigned to a road gang working outside the prison walls, he drew a gun he had managed to obtain and made off. (Another account has him walking away from the crew when the guards weren't paying attention.)

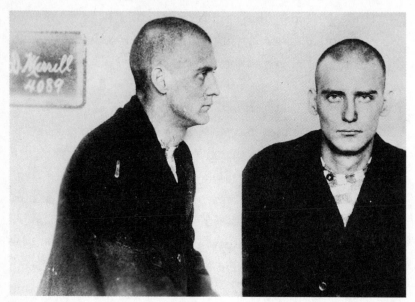

Dave Merrill.
Oregon State Archives

From there he was said to have gone to Colorado, committed a number of robberies with a partner named Lant, and then murdered a rancher. He was arrested for this crime and jailed but escaped. Arrested a second time and jailed again, he escaped a second time and disappeared.

Although there is no definitive proof, it has often been reported that he rode with Butch Cassidy and the Sundance Kid's Wild Bunch. This legend alternates between his being admired by the gang for his bravery or being thrown out for being too mean. Whether or not those stories are true, it is known that he rode the Rocky Mountains "outlaw trail" for a time in the 1890s.

At five feet, ten inches, with gray eyes, light hair, and a mustache, Tracy turned up in Portland, Oregon, in 1898. By the fall of that year he launched a spree of bold, daylight robberies along with partner Dave Merrill. Working right in the city, the two robbed butcher shops, grocery stores, drugstores, trolley

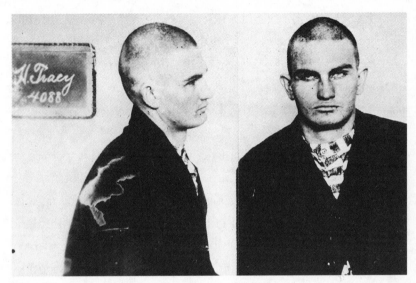

Harry Tracy.
Oregon State Archives

cars, and, especially, saloons, which they seemed to prefer as
marks more than other kinds of businesses. They often targeted
these businesses as soon as the establishments were opened for
business for the day and the proprietors least expected trouble.

Their modus operandi was straightforward and brutal.
They would burst into the shop or saloon and demand money
or other valuables from the clerk or customers or threaten them
with a beating if they caused any trouble. Sometimes they
would bind and gag their victims if they didn't cooperate to the
bandits' satisfaction. Tracy and Merrill usually wore costume
masks during their holdups to disguise their identities, gaining
them the nickname the False Face Bandits.

Tracy was a shrewd and careful outlaw who knew how to
keep his mouth shut. Merrill wasn't, and took to bragging of his
and Tracy's banditry exploits in the Portland saloons and flop-
houses. Other patrons were overhearing what he had to say and
eventually word got around to the Portland Police Department.

The Portland police had been anxious for the opportunity to introduce themselves to the False Face Bandits and put an end to the terror they were causing the fair city's honest merchants. Detectives Cordano, Ford, and Weiner were put on the case, and late one night in February 1899, they followed Merrill home from a local bar.

Upon searching his house, they discovered a variety of stolen goods and arrested him. A couple of days later, when Tracy dropped by, the detectives were waiting. Tracy spotted them and ran for it. A brief gunfight on the streets of Portland ensued. Even a bystander, Albert Wey, who was said to have been a past victim of Tracy and Merrill, got in on the action by firing a shotgun at the outlaw as he dashed by, detectives in hot pursuit. But the jig was up and Tracy was soon captured. Within a few months, both Tracy and Merrill were at the Oregon State Penitentiary sporting prison stripes.

But three years later, as the smoke and confusion were still clearing from the prison yard on that June morning, Tracy and Merrill were carefully making their way to the last place the authorities would expect them to go—Salem.

It's unlikely that the identity of whoever supplied Tracy and Merrill with their rifles will ever be known. One theory says that Tracy's wife, Mollie, was somehow able to smuggle them in, or arranged to have someone else smuggle them in. It is known that Tracy once wrote a letter to her asking for such a favor, but she refused. Perhaps later she had a change of heart? Prison Warden J. T. Janes felt that Tracy and Merrill had made some kind of deal with an ex-con named Harry Wright, with whom they had been acquainted in prison. Janes theorized that, since Wright knew his way around the penitentiary, he could have easily managed to get in, hide the weapons, and sneak out again. There is some doubt about each of these theories, but no doubt about the fact that two rifles were hidden in the foundry that morning and Tracy and Merrill knew exactly when and where to find them.

Slipping into the city after dark, their first stop was at the home of a J. W. Roberts, from whom they took some civilian clothes to replace their prison duds. Heading north, they stole a team of Clydesdale horses that had been secured for the night in a barn just outside of the city. Dressed to blend in with the general populace, they made toward the small farm community of Gervais, about ten miles north of Salem.

By now, the alarm had been sounded, and Marion County Sheriff Durbin had formed a posse to give chase. The prison warden, stung by the murders of three of his guards during the escape, offered a five hundred dollar reward for Tracy and Merrill's capture, dead or alive, then quickly raised it to one thousand dollars.

With about fifty men at his disposal and experienced bloodhounds and their expert handler on the way from the Washington State Penitentiary in Walla Walla to help with the search, Durbin expressed great confidence they would have their men in a couple of days. He would soon have a major change of attitude.

On the evening of the next day, June 10, Tracy and Merrill dropped in on Gervais resident Alonzo Biggs. With guns drawn, they forced him to cook them dinner, although what he prepared has not been recorded.

After filling their bellies, they left their unwilling dinner host and strolled into downtown Gervais. By now, the sheriff and his men had encircled the town, based on a number of reported sightings of the outlaws in the area, some of which were actually true. But the cagey cons weren't out of the game yet.

As they were wandering the downtown streets of Gervais, a buggy came rolling along. Inside rode several members of the sheriff's posse. Too good an opportunity to miss, Tracy and Merrill hopped aboard as they passed. Showing the startled and chagrined buggy occupants their rifles, the outlaws gave them the boot but not before helping themselves to the men's weapons. Casually driving the buggy through the sheriff's cordon and abandoning it down the road, the two escaped once more.

Before the two moved on from Gervais, there would be a couple of more taunts hurled at the sheriff and his posse. The morning after the buggy caper, Tracy and Merrill moseyed into the camp of August King, who was cutting firewood, and ordered him to make them breakfast. King complied, not knowing who they were until after they departed. After he reported the incident to the sheriff, the posse set the bloodhounds loose.

The posse, which now numbered more than two hundred men, set off behind the dogs and handler E. M. Carson. At one point they were sure they had the two cons trapped in a copse of trees near Gervais. They posted guards there all night to keep them buttoned up, but the early morning search revealed that the two had never been there.

While the posse was fruitlessly searching the timber stand, woodcutter August King looked up from his campfire and was astonished to see that the two outlaws had returned for a second breakfast. Tracy reportedly said to King, "I suppose you know who we are."

This time they paid him for his trouble.

Law enforcement authorities and politicians were beginning to become alarmed and embarrassed at the lack of progress being made in capturing the convicts. Oregon Governor T. Greer ordered three Oregon National Guard companies mobilized and posted along all major travel routes.

If the manhunters were not doing well, the newspapers were having a field day. Reporters and photographers followed the posse day and night, interviewing and photographing them and the people in the towns through which the outlaws passed, or were rumored to have passed. They issued daily reports of facts, speculation, and opinion that were read voraciously by readers throughout the country as they followed the saga. Tracy and Merrill were being quickly transformed from common criminals to the stuff of dime-novel heroes.

At one point during the pursuit, the *Seattle Daily Times* editorialized, "In all the criminal lore of the country there is no record equal to that of Harry Tracy for cold-blooded nerve, desperation and thirst for crime. Jesse James, compared with Tracy, is a Sunday school teacher."

Early on the morning of June 11, the men tracking Tracy and Merrill got a taste of how cold-blooded these two outlaws could be, even while on the run.

The bloodhounds, finally catching a scent, had led the posse to a stand of trees near Gervais. This time the two were really in there—they had been spotted earlier—and the posse was hot to move in for the capture. But Sheriff Durbin remained calm and professional and looked over the situation carefully. What he saw, he didn't like. A short distance into the trees was an opening lined by a pile of boulders, a good, sheltered place from which a couple of outlaws might stage an ambush. He was right. Tracy and Merrill were hunkered down behind those rocks waiting for their pursuers to come within range of their rifles.

Mindful of the potential for loss of life, the sheriff ordered his men to back off. He decided the best course of action was to have his men surround the fugitives and fire into the trees throughout the night to keep them pinned down and take them into custody in the morning. It was over as far as Durbin was concerned.

Dawn broke on June 12, and the posse nervously moved into the trees. It wasn't long before they realized that Tracy and Merrill weren't there. Somehow in the night the two had managed to slip through the ring of guards and were gone. At 7:30 a.m., Durbin got a phone call informing him that Tracy and Merrill had just breakfasted—in their usual manner as someone's uninvited guests—in the burg of Monitor, six miles away.

The posse, continuing on behind the bloodhounds, only occasionally found the trail or followed up on reports of sightings of the outlaws that were usually false alarms. In one odd incident, a rumor went around that Tracy had a sister nearby and had stopped to visit for a few days. The posse decided that it would be impolite to interrupt him while visiting family and neglected to investigate. When they finally decided that maybe they should have a look after all, Tracy and Merrill were reported to be in the town of Needy, far to the north.

By then, the searchers had exhausted all of their leads. The few times they had actually cornered Tracy and Merrill, the convicts had slipped away. Now the posse had no idea where to look. By June 14 they had pretty much given up and gone home.

The last reliable report of Tracy and Merrill in Oregon came on June 15. The fugitives had stolen two horses and a wagon near Oregon City and driven the rig over the Clackamas River to Fisher's Landing on the Columbia River. Here they commandeered a boat and boatman, whom they compelled to row them to the Washington State side of the river. Tracy and Merrill were now the problem of Durbin's Washington counterparts.

The two convicts continued their flight from the law in Washington, where things eventually began to break down.

Tracy, while perusing a newspaper article about the duo's exploits, was stunned to read that Merrill had set him up for his arrest in 1899 by telling the Portland police, in return for a shorter jail sentence, when Tracy was coming to visit. In a rage Tracy shot Merrill on June 28 near Chehalis, Washington, in a "duel" that involved Tracy turning and shooting Merrill in the back before the count was up.

Still hunted and still incorrigibly violent, Tracy killed three Washington law enforcement officers in shootouts—Deputy Sheriff Charles Raymond in Bothell and Seattle Police Officer E. E. Breese on July 3. On July 4 he wounded Seattle Deputy Game Warden Neil Rawley, who died the next day.

The reward for Tracy was now at eight thousand dollars. But the noose was finally closing. Alone now, Tracy ran east. On August 5, 1902, a posse cornered him near Creston, in eastern Washington. Shot several times, he crawled painfully into a cornfield and, rather than being captured, took out his revolver, placed the barrel against his head, and pulled the trigger. The manhunt was over.

Although Tracy and Merrill's breakout brought them death rather than freedom, their escape, ironically, resulted directly in one inmate's release. Frank Inghram, the fellow inmate who had tried to stop Tracy and Merrill on the morning of their escape, eventually had his leg amputated as the result of his gunshot wound. As a reward for his effort, the governor of Oregon gave the lifer a pardon, and he went home.

Tracy's body was returned to the Oregon State Penitentiary for burial. To discourage anyone from being tempted to dig up his body and use it for commercial display, authorities poured acid on his face to disfigure it and interred him in an unmarked grave on the prison grounds. Its location is unknown to this day.

The McCartys

Crime Runs in the Family

Digging a tunnel between the ranch house kitchen and the barn was an odd chore for a couple of Oregon cattlemen, but Tom and Bill McCarty weren't your typical ranchers, and this little project had nothing to do with raising livestock. The tunnel the two men were meticulously hollowing out beneath Bill's ranch in the Powder River Valley was part of a careful plan the two had been laying out over the winter of 1890–1891. And Tom and Bill were careful men.

If their subterranean activities were a little unusual, the fact that they were ranchers wasn't. They had grown up in a long-time ranching family that, over the years, had raised cattle in Utah, Montana, Nevada, California, and Oregon.

The movement of people from the East and Midwest to the West to take up farming and ranching was typical for the time period. But there were a couple of things about the McCarty family that made them a little different from many of their contemporaries. The first was they didn't much like company and crowds. They kept to themselves, lived far from settlements, and tended to move on when the country got too settled. What was more unusual was that the three sons, Tom, Bill, and George, found that a touch of larceny added a little spice to the ranching business (as well as helping to pay the bills). Now, as Tom and Bill worked on their tunnel, that brotherly penchant for crime was about to culminate in a bona fide family outlaw gang that would make its mark across the remote reaches of Oregon's Baker and Wallowa Counties.

By the time Tom McCarty, along with his brother-in-law, Matt Warner (Tom was married to Matt's sister for a time), showed up at brother Bill's Powder River ranch in Baker County sometime in 1890, most of the McCarty clan had relocated to Oregon, although Tom and Matt had left wives behind in Utah. Brother George, unlike the rest of the family, had been more interested in mining than ranching, and was living with his wife, Nellie, in the gold country near Cornucopia at the southern terminus of the Wallowa Mountains. One of the three McCarty sisters, Lois, was living in the area with her husband. The elder McCartys, who were law-abiding citizens all their lives, resided in Myrtle Point in the southwestern part of the state.

Of the three brothers, Tom was the oldest. He was about forty in 1890. He and his two brothers had operated a successful cattle ranch that had been founded by their father in Utah Territory. The three married during that period, and their parents relocated to Oregon to start a new ranch, leaving the old one to their sons. In 1884 the brothers sold the ranch for $35,000. Bill and George eventually moved to Baker County, Oregon, while Tom, the most inclined toward crime of the three, stayed behind and got into the cattle-rustling business with a little armed robbery thrown in.

By the late 1880s Tom and Matt Warner had fallen in with Butch Cassidy and his Wild Bunch gang of outlaws. In one of their most famous capers, Tom, Matt, and Butch robbed the bank in Telluride, Colorado, on June 24, 1889. Evidently wanting to make a good impression on the townsfolk, the three rode into Telluride wearing their best clothes. While Tom guarded the bank door, Warner and Cassidy rushed inside with their six-shooters cocked, readily talking the bank teller, a man named Hyde, into giving them a sack full of money. Outside of town Cassidy's brother,

Dan, and another gang member named Madden, were waiting with fresh horses. They all made their getaway $10,500 richer.

Several months earlier, on March 30, Tom McCarty had made a bit of a name for himself when he had marched into the Bank of Denver and insisted upon seeing David Moffat, the bank president. When Moffat appeared, McCarty held up a small liquid-filled bottle and told the agitated official that it was nitroglycerin. If he didn't hand over the bank's cash, he would reduce the establishment to a pile of toothpicks. The amount he walked out with is not known for certain. One unlikely story has it that Moffat wrote him a check for $23,000 and then personally cashed it for him.

But Tom and Matt's money started to run low after the Telluride robbery, and they were getting a little too well known in the whole Utah–Colorado–Wyoming area anyway. Tom thought they should take a ride to northeast Oregon where he had family and where there were plenty of fresh banks to rob. Brother-in-law Warner thought it over and decided that was not a bad idea.

When they arrived they found Bill glad to see them, but in some financial difficulty. Bill is thought to have been dabbling in horse stealing with Oregon outlaw and ex-brother-in-law Hank Vaughan (who was previously married to sister Lois). Nevertheless, money was tight and he, wife Lettie, sons Fred and Pearl, and stepson, Eck, were in grave danger of losing their thousand-acre ranch to creditors. When Tom and Matt proposed they form a gang to rob banks, Bill bought in quickly. Although Lettie, Eck, and Pearl would have nothing to do with the idea, seventeen-year-old Fred wanted in, too.

Next, they paid a visit to brother George, who also readily agreed to sign up. Much to everyone's surprise, his wife, Nellie, thought the idea of being in an outlaw gang was just grand, and she would also help. With brothers Bill and George aboard, along with brother-in-law Warner, sister-in-law Nellie, and nephew Fred, Tom had himself a gang knitted together not only by a lust for loot but by blood and marriage as well. They were going to make bank robbery a family affair.

Their first heist would be the Wallowa National Bank in Enterprise in the fall of 1891. Since coming to Oregon, Tom McCarty had envisioned an outlaw enterprise that robbed banks and trains and rustled cattle and horses throughout northeast Oregon and into Washington State. And this was good country for outlaws. With the rugged Wallowa Mountains to the east and the Blues to the west, the Powder River Valley and surrounding country were as remote as any place else in the West. Because the region was so wild in those days, outlaws on the run could travel unnoticed. It was also cattle country and gold country, two local products of special interest to McCarty. To Tom McCarty's way of thinking, it was just the sort of place that should have its own gang the way Wyoming, Colorado, and Utah had the Wild Bunch. In fact, Tom McCarty and Warner even made a trip to Wyoming sometime in 1891–1892 to look up their old compadre Butch Cassidy and invite him to join the McCarty Gang in Oregon. Butch wasn't interested.

His sights set on his own northeast Oregon outlaw empire, Tom had been making many advance preparations. Escape tunnels and hollowed-out haystacks—which would eventually serve Tom and Bill well—were prepared on Bill's ranch. Using money from his Colorado robberies, Tom also purchased strategically placed parcels of land and cabins in the area to function as hideouts, temporary holding areas for stolen cattle, and as way stations when the gang was on the run from the law.

With the gang assembled and a string of hideouts in place, the McCarty family was ready to take a little ride into

Enterprise. The robbery took place on the afternoon of October 8, 1891. Sporting beards, Matt (who was going by the name Raz Christiansen, his actual family name), Tom, and Bill rode into town dressed in their usual cowboy outfits. The rest of the gang was camped in a nearby meadow.

Tom took a position outside the bank door, just as he had when the Wild Bunch robbed the bank in Telluride, to keep any bank customers from entering. Matt and Bill walked inside. One of them approached the lone teller, W. R. Holmes, and inquired if there had been a deposit made for someone named Smith. Holmes replied there hadn't. But the cowboy at the window asked again and received the same answer. This time, a pistol was produced and the teller was ordered to hand over the money.

Startled, Holmes began to back away. Suddenly, the other bandit leaped over the counter, produced his six-shooter, and demanded the teller freeze. Bill and Matt shoved Holmes into his

Wallowa National Bank in Enterprise, Oregon, robbed by the McCarty gang.
Wallowa County Museum

office and ordered him to open the safe. Holmes protested that it was on a time lock and he couldn't. But the outlaws didn't buy his story and gave him the choice: Open the safe or die on the spot. The teller opened the safe and handed McCarty and Warner two bags of silver and a bag of gold worth about $3,500. Nervous, but still thinking fast, Holmes told the two there was no cash in the bank, resulting in their overlooking about six thousand dollars that was sitting on a nearby desk, covered with papers.

Meanwhile, some townsfolk, noting the commotion at the bank, were coming over to investigate. The bookkeeper of a nearby store, G. W. Hyatt, rushed over to see what was going on. Tom McCarty intercepted him at the door, knocked him down, and rapped him on the head with his pistol butt.

By the time Bill and Matt charged out of the bank and mounted their horses, a crowd had gathered. A young attorney named D. W. Sheahan came running over. Tom McCarty began shooting at his feet, making him dance a brief jig. Wheeling their mounts and firing in the air, Tom, Bill, and Matt rode south out of town on the Hurricane Creek Road. The locals made a disorganized attempt to form a posse and pursue the bandits—the three of whom would eventually be referred to as the Invincible Three—but gave up after only a short chase.

The McCarty family propensity for keeping to itself was paying off. No one recognized any of the robbers, and it would be years before it would become known that the not-yet-famous McCarty Gang had pulled off this job.

With their first family outing a great success, it was time for an encore. This time they decided on a night robbery of the bank in Summerville. At 9:00 p.m. on November 5, bank bookkeeper H. C. Rinehart was leaving after a long day's work. As he stepped out the door, Tom and Bill McCarty were waiting for him. Six-shooters drawn, they pushed him back inside and forced him to open the safe, which Rinehart did without resistance. The two outlaws ran off on foot with nearly five thousand dollars in cash. Bill's son Fred was waiting nearby with their horses. With the streets of the small frontier town deserted at that late hour and no one available to give chase, the McCartys rode off to one of their cabin hideouts unmolested.

The gang probably laid low over the winter of 1891–1892, enjoying the fruits of their labors, planning their next round of robberies, and perhaps even engaging in some legitimate ranching. It is also speculated that Tom and Bill continued to be involved with ex-brother-in-law Hank Vaughan stealing horses. Tom, being an old cattle rustler, probably continued those activities as well.

By spring 1892 they were back in action, this time with a plan to rob the patrons and gamblers at Baker City's ritzy Hotel Warshauer. It did not go quite as well as their last two capers. Bill and George casually strolled into the hotel one night, acting like any other guests. Tom and Matt were waiting outside in an alley, heavily armed. When the time was right, the outlaws inside the hotel would signal the two outside through a window. Tom and Matt would rush in and the foursome would relieve everyone of their valuables. According to the story, however, a policeman came along and, seeing Tom and Matt in the alley, took them to be vagrants. When he tried to arrest them, Tom hit the officer on the head with his rifle, knocking him out cold. All four outlaws left town in a hurry, empty-handed.

Licking their wounds from this unexpected failure, the gang decided to give train robbery a try. Unfortunately for the gang, this endeavor was not destined to go much better.

In late April they piled logs and rocks on the Union Pacific Railroad tracks between North Powder and Telocaset. The

The rugged mountains of northeastern Oregon where the McCarty gang
hid from the law.
Baker County Library Historic Photo Collection

strategy was simple. When a train came along, it would be
stopped so the tracks could be cleared. The engineer, thinking a
landslide had caused the blockade, would not be suspicious that
there was something funny afoot. But when the train came by
late that afternoon, it didn't stop. The engineer opened up the
throttle, the train's cowcatcher easily cleared the way for him,
and the train disappeared down the tracks.

A few days later they hit a combination store and bank in
Sparta, a nearby gold-mining camp, with considerably more success. Since it lacked the security of a regular bank, the McCartys
could easily take it. Bill, Tom, and Matt disguised themselves
with red bandanas and fake whiskers made from horsehair.
Entering the store, they ordered the few customers inside to put
their hands up and stand in a line, while the clerk was compelled
to open the safe and hand over gold nuggets and cash.

The Hotel Warshauer, which the McCartys attempted to rob.
Baker County Library Historic Photo Collection

All was going just fine until they turned to leave. On the way out, Bill McCarty spotted a display of cowboy boots for sale and decided he needed a new pair. As Tom and Matt looked on with impatience, Bill sat down and began trying on different styles and sizes as if he were pleasure shopping on a lazy afternoon. At one point a customer walked into the shop, unaware that a robbery was transpiring, and was knocked to the ground before he could turn and run. With that, the three thought they had better get going. Bill grabbed a pair of boots he decided would suit him the best and followed his two fellow outlaws out the door. A safe few miles away, Bill stopped to take a closer look at his new merchandise only to realize that instead of two new boots he had taken one new one and one of his old ones—and they were both for left feet!

Returning to Bill's ranch riding fresh horses supplied by George and Nellie, the gang hid the nuggets in the chicken coop until they could sell them out of the area where word of the Sparta robbery hadn't traveled.

Nearly a month later, when Bill went out to the chicken coop to check on the nuggets, he found them gone. The mystery was solved when son Fred showed up wearing a fancy new set of clothes. He had found the nuggets, gone to Boise, Idaho, sold them for six hundred dollars, and then gone on a shopping spree. When Fred explained what he had done, father and uncle just laughed. He was a real McCarty, after all.

By the summer of 1892, the McCarty Gang had pulled off a number of robberies throughout northeast Oregon. Tom got to thinking they needed to try out some new territory for a while until things cooled down in Baker and Wallowa Counties.

The gang headed up to central Washington and bought a ranch for seven hundred dollars they called the 7 U, setting themselves up as legitimate cattlemen for a time. The real purpose of the ranch, of course, was as a base of operations for more robberies. From here they made a failed attempt to rob Forepaugh's Circus, which was performing in Moscow, Idaho. The gang also

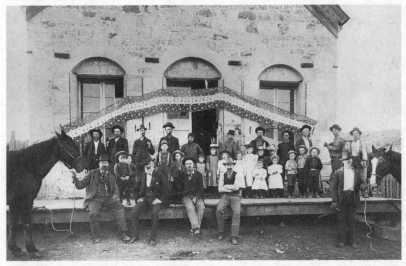

Sparta Store robbed by McCartys.
Baker County Library Historic Photo Collection

successfully robbed banks in Wenatchee and Roslyn, Washington, in 1892, where, reportedly, Tom shot a man in the stomach. But there was big trouble for the gang looming on the horizon.

Matt Warner's wife, Rose, whom he had left behind in Utah and not seen in some time, eventually came to live with him in Oregon, then moved to the 7 U Ranch when the family relocated there. (Tom's wife refused an invitation to come.) After a time Rose began to complain that she was getting lonely while he and the rest of the gang were out robbing. Rose convinced Matt to bring her sister Sara Jane in from Utah to keep her company. It was a decision he would come to regret.

Unlike Rose, Sara Jane did not approve of their outlaw activities and, apparently, did not like brother-in-law Matt very much either. Shortly after the Roslyn bank robbery, Sara Jane went back to Utah. In spite of her promise to keep what she knew about the McCarty Gang to herself, she went to the police in Salt Lake City and told all. Warrants were issued for the McCarty Gang, and in April 1893 Matt Warner and George McCarty found themselves in jail awaiting trial. Matt was arrested at a small tent restaurant he operated with Rose in Beasley Springs, Washington, and George at his mining claim near Sumpter, Oregon. Both were arrested without incident and transferred to the Kittitas County jail in Ellensburg, Washington.

To pay for their defense, legend has it that Matt Warner drew a map to where the outlaws had hidden $41,000 in ill-gotten cash. When the lawyers were done, Matt and George were freed due to lack of evidence, and only five hundred dollars were left of the original forty-one grand.

The law had come after Bill, Fred, and Tom McCarty also, but without success. When the arrest warrants were issued, Baker County Sheriff Porter Conde rode out to Bill's Powder

River Valley ranch to try and take them alone. Instead he was met by Tom's Winchester rifle. It turned him back, empty-handed and lucky to escape with his skin still intact.

The McCarty Gang had become a little too famous in Oregon, and it was time to move on. After hiding in a hollowed-out haystack, the three men made their way to Tom's old haunts in Colorado. The end of the McCarty Gang was drawing near.

Tom, Bill, and Fred McCarty rode into the town of Delta on September 6, 1893. They were planning to make a withdrawal from the Farmers and Merchants Bank. Before taking action, they decided to look around a little first. They had lunch at an establishment called Bricktops on Main Street and dinner at another place called Central House.

Early the next morning they hid their horses in an alley and walked down to the bank. Once inside, Tom pulled his gun on a bank lawyer as he sat at his desk. Fred jumped over the railing from the lobby into the counting room while Bill kept an eye on things, gun at the ready.

The bank cashier, A. T. Blachley, shouted a loud warning that the bank was being robbed, hoping that someone in the street would hear. He was told sharply to keep quiet. He yelled again. This time, one of the McCartys shot Blachley twice in the head and he fell to the floor dead. Bill and Fred stuffed the cash in their shirts as Tom continued to keep his revolver trained on the surviving bank employees and customers.

Mission accomplished, the three ran out the door and made for their horses. But the usual McCarty luck had abandoned them. Local hardware dealer W. Ray Simpson had heard the shot that killed Blachley and come running with his .44 Sharps repeating rifle. Seeing what was happening, Simpson took aim at Bill McCarty as he mounted his horse and pulled the trigger. The bullet hit Bill in the back of the head and he slid, lifeless, off his horse. The next shot caught son Fred in the chest. He was dead before he hit the ground. The third shot was directed at Tom but went wide. Tom McCarty, his horse at full gallop, sped out of town. A posse, organized by Sheriff Girardet, made a valiant attempt to catch him but lost his trail somewhere on the Uncompahgre Plateau.

Back in Delta, the money was retrieved from the outlaws' shirts and returned to the bank. The bodies of Bill and Fred were photographed and buried in the same pine box in the local cemetery. A relative from Utah eventually identified the two from the photographs. The McCarty Gang would never ride again.

As for the rest of the McCarty Gang, George and Nellie moved to Idaho where they finally hit a vein of gold. Although involved in the robberies, Nellie was never charged with a crime. Matt Warner went back to Utah to ranch, but got in a little trouble and spent 1896 to 1900 in prison in Utah. After getting out, he went straight and even worked for a time as a deputy sheriff. He died in 1938 in Price, Utah.

Some say that Tom McCarty returned to northeast Oregon and worked in honest jobs for Wallowa County and the US Forest Service and then died in obscurity with his neighbors never suspecting his real identity. Another theory has him committing suicide in Denver. But the last time Tom McCarty was seen for certain was on the morning of September 7, 1893, as he vanished into the vastness of Colorado's plateau country.

Even if Tom McCarty never did return to Baker and Wallowa Counties, there are reminders of him and his family in place names that dot the map of that country—McCarty Springs, McCarty Bridge, McCarty Creek, McCarty Horse Camp—enduring reminders of Oregon's outlaw family.

Dave Tucker

From Bank Robbery to Redemption

Dave Tucker was an upstanding citizen in the northeast Oregon ranching community of Joseph. How could the vice president of the Joseph State Bank be anything else? Before that, he was a respected businessman, rancher, and farmer. And before that, he had worked tending and shearing sheep until he earned enough money to start his own sheep and cattle business. What more respectable a background could a man raised in the wild, frontier days of Wallowa County have?

If you were to have walked into the Joseph State Bank to do business with Tucker, you would have found him honest and forthright—a pleasure to work with. But when you shook his hand to seal the deal, you probably would have noticed that his "trigger finger" was missing. That's because before Dave Tucker had gone respectable, he'd been a bank robber whose finger had been blown off during a getaway shootout. The bank he robbed, thirty-two years earlier in 1896, was the very one of which he had just been made vice president.

The Wallowa County of the late 1800s was very different from the one Tucker lived in now. His family came to the Wallowa Valley in 1877, and Dave was one of several boys in a large family of brothers and sisters. His father, a veteran of the Civil War, settled his brood on a homestead along Prairie Creek.

This was wild country in those days with lots of wilderness and few roads. Farming, cattle and sheep ranching, and timbering

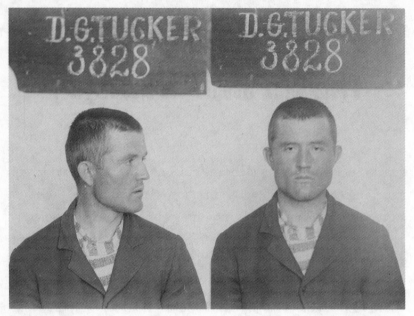

Dave Tucker.
Oregon State Archives

were the main occupations. The setting and the landscape were, as they are today, breathtaking, with the jagged peaks of the Wallowa Mountains towering above the immense Wallowa Valley.

Dave Tucker attended school for a short time and regularly worked with his father on the ranch. When his father could spare him, he worked for another rancher, Peter Beaudoin, herding and shearing sheep. When he sheared sheep, it was said, he carried with him a Bible that was given to him by former schoolmate and sweetheart Minnie Proebstel, whom he would later marry.

But some contemporaries have written that the Tucker boys could be trouble. Dave had a little trouble early on when he was charged with stealing a calf—a charge he vigorously denied—and sentenced to a year at the Oregon State Penitentiary. Out of prison, he was embittered and resentful of the experience, and it gave him a poor attitude. Nevertheless, when he got out of jail, he went back to work at his former occupation in the sheep camps.

Sometime in the summer of 1896, when Tucker was twenty-five years old, a couple of drifters wandered into the Wallowa Valley from Idaho. They were James Brown and Cyrus Fitzhugh, and had come to visit the wife of a Wallowa County homesteader to whom Fitzhugh was related. After visiting for a short time, the men took jobs in local sheep camps. This is probably where they met Dave Tucker.

Somewhere during the course of their long hours of labor, Fitzhugh suggested that they rob the First Bank of Joseph. Fitzhugh claimed to have experience at this sort of thing, having robbed a payroll in Montana. He also lied and said that he had been a member of the McCarty Gang that had held up the bank in Enterprise in 1891. Tucker felt he had a score to settle with society and told Fitzhugh and Brown to count him in.

In 1896 Joseph had only been an official town with a post office for sixteen years. It was a typical remote frontier community of the day, with just a handful of buildings, including, of course, a bank and several saloons. Even in such a small ranch town, robbing a bank required some advance planning, and the three men began meeting at Martin's Saloon in Joseph to plot the details. Over the course of a couple of months, saloon owner John Martin and his bartender, Ben Ownbey, were drawn into the scheme.

It's difficult to say why the latter two men joined in. Martin was a successful and well-known businessman in town, and business was reputed to be good. Ownbey, in his mid-thirties, was a former deputy sheriff and deputy county clerk in Enterprise about seven miles to the north. After losing his last political job in the 1890 local election, he moved to the outskirts of Joseph with his wife and three children and took a job at the saloon.

Finally, after many evenings around bottles of beer and glasses of whiskey, the plan was ready for execution—the date set for October 1, 1896. They estimated they would make off with about six thousand dollars, assuming that the bank would be holding cash brought in by ranchers from the sale of the season's lamb crop. But as the date approached, Ownbey developed cold feet and wanted out. He got no sympathy from ringleader Fitzhugh who told him if he tried to back out now he would "get him." Ownbey considered going to the bank and warning them about the impending heist, but figured Tucker, Fitzhugh, Brown, and Martin would just deny it and maybe murder him in retaliation. So he kept his mouth shut, but vowed to play as little a role in the robbery as possible.

Reports say that October 1, 1896, was one of those warm, gorgeous autumn days, with a clear blue sky and the aspens and cottonwoods resplendent in their gold-leaved glory. J. D. McCully, who was a cashier at the bank and a clerk at the McCully Store across the street, had been dividing his time between the two businesses all day long, locking the door of the bank when he left. Unknown to him, that afternoon Dave Tucker was casually hanging around in the street outside the bank, watching and waiting for McCully to open the doors once again.

At about 2:30 p.m. McCully unlocked the bank doors so he could attend to some customers' business. That was just what Tucker had been waiting for. He walked across the street and then back again—a predetermined signal for Fitzhugh and Brown, who were mounted on their horses and watching from a distance down the street, that the bank doors were open. (Another version has Ownbey giving the signal by walking across the street wearing a red bandana around his neck.)

The bank was ripe for plucking. Fitzhugh and Brown rode purposefully down the dusty street, jumped off their horses, tied

First Bank of Joseph, Oregon.
Wallowa County Museum

them to the hitching post, and ran into the bank with six-shooters drawn. They wore bandana masks and black soot rubbed on their faces to disguise their identities. One of them also carried a shotgun. Inside, along with cashier McCully, they found four bank customers—three women and one man who carried no weapon.

McCully was in the bank vault when the outlaws entered. They were so quiet that he didn't hear them and only realized the two interlopers were there when he walked out of the vault to see a couple of revolvers aimed in his direction.

"Throw up your hands," one of the masked men ordered.

As he believed it was a joke, McCully's first reaction was to laugh. But a closer inspection of those guns and the grim, disguised faces behind them made McCully realize this was no prank. It was a real bank robbery.

Outside, Tucker stood at the bank entrance with his revolver drawn, stopping anybody who passed by and keeping them there so as not to run off and sound the alarm. Own-bey stood alongside Tucker, but was not armed. John Martin appears not to have been at the scene of the robbery at all.

Before long, Tucker and Ownbey had a small crowd held hostage in front of the bank. Inside, Fitzhugh and Brown were stuffing cash and gold into a sack, while threatening McCully with death if he tried anything funny. In about ten minutes the two robbers had found all the cash and gold they could, a disappointing two thousand dollars, and moved toward the door, using McCully as a shield. Once outside, the bandits got something they hadn't factored into their plans—a shootout.

Despite Tucker and Ownbey's efforts to keep a lid on the robbery in progress, the unusual situation of a crowd stand-ing around in front of the bank was arousing suspicion among the townsfolk, many of whom were armed. One man who quickly figured out what was going on was rancher Fred Wag-ner. Standing behind his wagon in front of the McCully Store, Wagner picked up his .45-70 Winchester rifle and waited for the outlaws to show themselves. As they came out the door, he began firing. Another man commenced shooting from the upstairs window of a nearby building.

McCully dived to the ground as bullets whizzed by and ric-ocheted off the bank's front wall. Brown was hit before he got off the bank steps, falling backwards and landing in a sitting position with his head and shoulders propped against the bank wall, dead.

Bullets flew everywhere. Fitzhugh and Tucker, in a state of confusion and shock, began to fire back wildly but without fatal result. Brown had been carrying the bag of cash and gold, which now lay by his body directly in the path of withering gunfire. Fitzhugh, without hesitation, dashed for the treasure. Grabbing it while still firing his six-shooter and dodging the slugs meant for him, he ran to his horse. The town blacksmith tried to grab the horse away from the outlaw, but Fitzhugh knocked him aside. Holding onto the saddle horn, Fitzhugh hung on as his steed bucked up and down across the street. Swinging into the saddle, he reined his horse to the east and sped out of town with the sack of loot slung over his shoulder. On his way, he encountered a man walking down the street, a Southerner who had fought in the Civil War on the side of the Confederates. Fitzhugh shot at his feet to scare him, but it just made the gent, who was uncharacteristically unarmed that day, mad. Fitzhugh supposedly gave him instructions to tell the crowd at the bank "they can put their hands down now." With that, Fitzhugh rode off.

Meanwhile, back at the corner bank, things were still pretty hot. Dave Tucker had taken a bullet in his right hand, causing his revolver to go flying and hopelessly mangling his right index finger. Unarmed and bleeding, Dave Tucker ran. Then, from out of the Post Office came local resident Alex Donnely with his shotgun. He fired it at Tucker as he sprinted away, and the pellets caught him in the side. Tucker staggered but kept going. With an angry crowd following him, he only got a couple of blocks.

Their first instinct was to string Tucker up on the spot. Upon further consideration, the crowd decided, since he was a local boy, to turn him over to Sheriff E. J. Forsythe instead. Tucker was lodged in the jail in Enterprise.

Ben Ownbey miraculously slipped off unscathed during the confusion of the getaway shootout. He and John Martin were arrested later when Tucker confessed to the crime and implicated his accomplices.

No trace of Fitzhugh could be found. It has been speculated that he stayed briefly at a friend's ranch near the upper Imnaha River and then crossed the Snake River into Idaho.

On April 21, 1897, Dave Tucker received a seven-year prison sentence at the Oregon State Penitentiary for his role in the robbery. Ben Ownbey got a slightly more lenient penalty because he was unarmed and played a less active role in the crime than Tucker. John Martin hired a Union County lawyer named Carroll for seven hundred dollars and was acquitted. James Brown's body was buried in the Hurricane Creek Cemetery. Legend has it that the young man had a sweetheart in the area who planted on his grave a rosebush that grew and bloomed for many years. Cyrus Fitzhugh and the two thousand dollars in cash and gold were never located. Fred Wagner received a gold watch from the First Bank of Joseph for his role in foiling the robbery.

While in prison, Tucker had ample time to mull over his mistakes. Determined to use his time as constructively as possible, he dropped the tough attitude, eventually to become a model prisoner and trusty.

Released after four and a half years for good behavior, Tucker returned to his home in the Wallowa Valley to try to rebuild his life. He started working, once again, for sheep grower Peter Beaudoin. In a few years he saved up enough of a grubstake to buy a small number of lambs that he eventually parlayed into a herd of cattle and sheep and a twelve-hundred-acre ranch. He married his childhood sweetheart, Minnie Proebstel, in 1906. His fortunes grew and his business prospered. He became known for the kindness and generosity he showed to his neighbors. It was said, "No one ever came to Dave Tucker for help that didn't get it." He hired those who needed work and gave a few bucks to those who were broke or in dire straits. He had literally transformed his life.

This full and remarkable circle was completed in 1928 when Dave Tucker was elected vice president of the Joseph State Bank

Peter Beaudoin, on the left, and Dave Tucker, on the right.
Wallowa County Museum

(formerly the First Bank of Joseph), the same establishment that he had robbed of two thousand dollars three decades before.

Years later, sitting in his bank office, Tucker must have sometimes cast his mind back to that beautiful October 1896 day and wondered how he had ever come to be standing before the bank door with revolver in hand. Perhaps he would idly wonder what became of Cyrus Fitzhugh and the two thousand dollars. Maybe he recalled his anger and bitterness that Fitzhugh had escaped with the loot and left him missing a finger and serving time in prison. But it didn't matter anymore. All these years later, it was Dave Tucker, not Cyrus Fitzhugh, who had ended up with the real treasure.

Hank Vaughan

"It's Pretty Hard to Kill Me Off."

Sudden shootouts between men with itchy trigger fingers were not a rare occurrence in the nineteenth-century frontier towns of eastern Oregon. Arguments during card games, business deals gone bad, or just plain grudges were all part of the mix. Weapons were as commonplace as horses and cowboy hats in those days, with frontier residents favoring arms such as the Sharps repeating rifle, .45 caliber Colt Army and Navy model revolvers, or the .44 Colt Dragoon revolver, a four-pound hand cannon guaranteed to stop anything in its tracks. When tempers flared among men packing six-shooters, the sound of gunshots often followed.

Sometimes the gunfights were fair and sometimes they weren't. Either way, they usually happened on the spur of the moment, fast, and up close and personal. Sometimes an armed man would shoot an unarmed one, and there was always the black art of the bushwhack. The law's response to gunplay was equally varied. The survivor of an impromptu gun duel might find himself under arrest and in the local jail, awaiting trial. If he could prove it was self-defense, he'd probably be released. If not, a cell at the Oregon State Penitentiary would be his destination. If the deceased happened to have a lot of friends in town, a vigilance committee might pay the jail a visit and, with a little rope and a conveniently located tree, take care of the whole affair itself. On the other hand, in some of the wilder towns and mining camps, nobody particularly cared who shot whom.

Hank Vaughan.
Bowman Museum and Crook County Historical Society

There are plenty of examples of shootings in Oregon frontier towns. Burns, down in Harney County, was a center for gunplay action. This is where Til Glaze, a saloon owner from Prineville, was shot and killed in a dispute over a horse race. In 1886 Pete Stenger died in a Burns gunfight with Rush Frazier, who had been making passes at his wife.

If interpersonal relations could be a mite touchy in frontier Oregon, so could being an employer. In the 1860s Grant County miner William Kane shot his boss to death, dumping his body in a sluice box where it floated away downstream. What got Kane so agitated was that on payday he had found himself being handed paper money instead of gold dust. Nobody in the county took paper money. Neither could it be converted to gold. His "pay" had been equal to only about forty cents on the dollar. If his boss was miserly about handing out gold, Kane was happy to present him with a generous dose of lead. Unfortunately, things did not work out quite as well as Kane might have wanted. He was arrested by Grant County Sheriff Frank McDaniels, tried for murder, convicted, and hanged.

One of the most famous Oregon frontier shootings was the murder of Peter French, overseer of one of the state's largest cattle empires. In the process of gaining control of a huge portion of Harney County, he had made more than a few enemies among his neighbors. He was known to fence off public domain lands and illegally acquire other properties. A move that especially angered his neighbors was a lawsuit he filed attempting to prevent settlers from owning some lands near Malheur Lake, which threatened their livelihoods.

On December 26, 1897, French was directing a cattle drive on his property when homesteader Ed Oliver came riding up to him at high speed. Oliver reined his horse in near French's, crashing the two animals into each other. French slashed at Oliver with his whip. The homesteader drew his revolver, shot the cattle baron in the head, and then turned and galloped off, leaving French lying dead on the ground.

But vigilantism could sometimes work in reverse. Oliver was initially charged with murder, which was later reduced to manslaughter. At the trial it took the sympathetic jury barely three hours to find Oliver not guilty.

While most shootings and shootouts on the frontier tended to be one-time events for the participants—especially the loser—some people made a habit of it.

In Oregon's semilawless northeast quarter, Hank Vaughan's Wild West career, at its most colorful, was a mix of gunplay, murder, livestock rustling, and occasional bouts of what resembled good citizenship.

Hank Vaughan was born on April 27, 1849, in the Waldo Hills near Eugene. As with many pioneer residents of the verdant Willamette Valley, his family farmed and ranched. By the early 1860s the clan had moved east of the Cascade Mountains, first to The Dalles and then further east to Canyon City in the Blue Mountains gold country where they supplied cattle to feed the hungry miners. It was here in 1864 that Vaughan, who was now fifteen years old, shot his first man.

The shooting involved a miner named William Headspot who, it has been speculated, bought a horse from Vaughan but couldn't come up with the full agreed-upon price. Observers at the scene saw the two arguing. The next moment, Vaughan, perhaps a little emboldened by alcohol, went for his revolver and shot Headspot dead.

The gold camps of that era were pretty rough places. Shootings and fistfights were regular occurrences. Since Canyon City was no exception, no one cared if there was one less miner around, and Vaughan went about his business as if nothing had happened.

In addition to whatever other occupations Vaughan engaged in while prowling northeast Oregon, horse stealing and cattle rustling seemed to be his favorites. These habits got him and his propensity to go for his gun into his first real trouble.

He and a friend named Dick Bunten had stolen some horses in Union County and, in the spring of 1865, were herding them to Idaho to sell. Along the way the two stopped to camp near the Express Ranch along the Burnt River in Baker County. Unknown to the two horse thieves, Union County Sheriff Frank Maddock, along with Deputy Sheriff O. J. Hart, had been hot on their trail.

Locating the horse thieves' camp, the two lawmen sat tight until the hour was late. Assuring themselves that Vaughan and Bunten were asleep, they quietly stole into camp under cover of darkness. Approaching the tent carefully with their revolvers drawn, Maddock suddenly called out to the two sleepers that the law had the drop on them and to come out with their hands up.

They came out of their tent all right—shooting furiously. Vaughan shot Deputy Sheriff Hart dead almost immediately, even as Bunten fell fatally wounded by the lawmen's gunfire. Now it was just Vaughan and Maddock firing at each other. One of Vaughan's slugs went through Maddock's cheek just as Vaughan was hit from the sheriff's return fire. Swinging the butt of his gun, Vaughan connected with Maddock's head, putting him out cold. The sheriff survived the incident, although not without some facial disfigurement. Vaughan galloped off into the night.

Traveling slowly because of his wound, Vaughan was easily captured by a posse within a few days and taken to Auburn for trial. Charged with murder and theft, he was sentenced to life in prison on May 29, 1865. While he was housed in the

Canyon City, site of Hank Vaughan's first shoot-out.
Grant County Historical Museum

Auburn jailhouse awaiting transfer to the Oregon State Penitentiary, a crowd of vigilantes gathered outside with a mind to change the sentence to death by hanging. This probably made Vaughan more than a little nervous. He had surely heard of the brutal lynching of Tom the Spaniard by an Auburn mob just three years earlier. The good folks of Auburn, a mining town in the Powder River Valley, had a reputation for taking the law into their own hands. Fortunately for Vaughan, there were apparently some people present who thought his legal penalty was just, and they were able to calm and disperse the mob.

Vaughan was taken to the Oregon State Penitentiary, which, in 1865, was located in Portland. The following year, the state penitentiary was relocated to Salem, and Vaughan and fellow prisoners went with it. Because of his good behavior while in prison, he was paroled in February 1870 at the age of twenty-one.

After his release, Vaughan wandered down to Nevada for a few years, perhaps working as a blacksmith, a trade he learned in

prison. Others claim he drove the family cattle herd there to sell
to miners working the Silver State mines. He may have also been
involved in murderous activities during his Nevada residency, as
well as a shootout with law officers in Prescott, Arizona, in which
a companion was killed. It was during this period that he also may
have met members of the infamous outlaw family the McCartys.
He would eventually marry one of the McCarty sisters, Lois.

Whatever his real business endeavors during this period, he
returned to eastern Oregon again in 1878, working with partners
Bill Moody and Still Heulet in the horse-trading business. They
typically traded in a mix of legally and illegally obtained animals. The method of choice for rustling, both horses and cattle,
involved riding the range and simply picking up animals that had
strayed from the main herd. In the largely unpopulated country of
northeast Oregon, the odds of getting caught in the act were small.

From horse thieves to bank robbers, the frontier mining towns of Oregon
attracted a certain kind of lawlessness.
Grant County Historical Museum

They did have some close calls, however. While corralling some stolen horses one day, Vaughan and Moody were set upon by a vigilance committee out looking for rustlers. The two holed up in a nearby barn, trading shots with the posse until nightfall when they managed to slip away.

The horse peddlers sold their stock to miners in Oregon and Idaho and later to the railroads, which needed animals to haul equipment and supplies to rail-line construction sites. It was said that, at its peak, the Vaughan–Moody–Heulet horse trading empire ranged from eastern Washington through northeast Oregon, southern Idaho, and into northern Nevada.

Hank Vaughan eventually wandered into the Crooked River country around Prineville in 1881, just before the Prineville vigilante wars broke out. He hung around for a while drifting, gambling, and indulging in the heavy drinking that would transform him from a friendly and easy-going companion into a dangerous, unpredictable gunfighter. It was here in Prineville that he had his most famous shootout—with a member of the notorious Prineville vigilante gang, no less.

It was a December day in 1881, and Hank Vaughan had stopped in at Til Glaze's saloon in Prineville to have a few drinks to ward off the winter chill. In the course of his libations, he got into a card game with Charley Long, who was, like himself, a gunfighter as well as a member of the vigilante gang that had begun to form in the area.

Vaughan and Long played cards for some time, talking and drinking. Then fellow saloon patrons began to detect a growing disagreement. It eventually escalated into a serious argument. No one knows for sure what the two gunslingers were arguing about, but legend has it that it was over which one of them was quicker and deadlier with a six-shooter. It finally came to a challenge.

Vaughan and Long laid their cards down and pushed their chairs back from the table. They walked to the center of the saloon as other patrons looked on nervously. The two men each grabbed one end of a long bandana with their left hands, then drew their pistols and began shooting. At such a close distance, every shot hit its mark. Long pulled the trigger first, the slug creasing Vaughan's scalp. Long shot again, this time hitting Vaughan in his left breast above the heart. When the smoke cleared, both were wounded but, miraculously, not fatally. Vaughan's friends carried the wounded man down the street to Dick Graham's saloon, where he was sure he was going to die. He recovered just fine.

So did Long, although his days as a gunfighter were numbered. After the vigilante gang was defeated and scattered in 1884, he went up to Washington State where he began bullying a local rancher, claiming he was going to take his ranch from him. One day the rancher hid behind a door and, when Long walked by, stepped out and shot him dead.

Because of Vaughan's notoriety, word of the Prineville shootout traveled fast throughout northeast Oregon. The reports that were circulating said Vaughan was severely wounded and certainly a goner.

The *Pendleton East Oregonian,* in his home territory, and the *Walla Walla* [Washington] *Statesman* both reported on his demise and expressed no regret at his presumed passing. Vaughan was outraged when he read the uncomplimentary tone of his obituaries. Once back on his feet, he stormed into the offices of the *East Oregonian* and ran editor J. P. Wagner and his staff out into the streets of Pendleton.

Vaughan had something of a dual personality, ruled mostly by how much alcohol he had imbibed. Not a big, imposing man, he weighed between 140 and 150 pounds and was inclined to dress nattily. Some type of armament was always part of his ensemble. In a good mood and sober, he was said to be friendly, personable, and reasonable. In a drunk, though, you better not look at him cross-eyed—or maybe not at all.

One of his favorite pranks, when he had had more than a few too many, was to randomly pick out someone in a saloon whom he thought might put on a good show and invite him to dance for the crowd by firing at the unfortunate innocent's feet. While that sort of stunt usually brought laughs from onlookers, it wasn't without its risks, even for an experienced gunman like Hank Vaughan.

Vaughan had a little trouble with one of his practical joke victims one afternoon in early August 1886. He'd been relaxing in the Blue Front Saloon in Centerville (now Athena). A stranger was also in the saloon having a couple of drinks. Vaughan looked him over and decided he would make a good subject for some sport. In his usual manner Vaughan stood up, drew his revolver, aimed at the gentleman's feet, and invited him to do a jig for the patrons. The stranger, Bill Falwell, wasn't going to indulge Vaughan, and told him so.

That was a mistake on Falwell's part. Hank Vaughan wasn't going to let anyone get the better of him any day of the week, let alone in front of a barroom audience. Vaughan slowly cocked the hammer of his pistol and began shooting. That changed Falwell's mind in a hurry, and he put on quite a dance for the laughing and hooting crowd.

Now it was Falwell's move. Decidedly unhappy with the humiliation he had been forced to endure, the newcomer walked out into the streets of Centerville and went to get himself a pistol. The story goes that he traded his horse to a local for a .50 caliber revolver. The next day he went looking for Hank Vaughan.

Falwell found him at about 6:00 p.m. in the Hollis & Cleve mercantile doing a little shopping. Without a word, Falwell began shooting, hitting Vaughan in the chest and right arm. As Vaughan dived for cover behind boxes of merchandise, Falwell kept firing until all six shots were gone. Leaving Vaughan wounded and bleeding, he ran off.

Vaughan was taken to Pendleton for medical attention. He recovered from his wounds, although his right arm did not work quite as well as it used to, requiring him to learn how to shoot with his left. One story has it that a lawyer, visiting his home in Centerville not long after the incident, found him practicing with his left arm by firing into a pile of pillows placed at the far end of his office.

Falwell was arrested for his assault on Vaughan and was sentenced to four years in the Oregon State Penitentiary.

In addition to his tendency toward six-shooter negotiations, Vaughan liked to ride fast as well, and was involved in a number of horse and buggy accidents over the years. Shooting up local landmarks and riding his horse through saloons also made up his repertoire of personal amusements.

Hank Vaughan's wild behavior and stunts provoked ambivalent feelings wherever he lived. For the local lawman, he could be problematic to deal with, depending on his mood and whether he was drunk or sober. One Umatilla County sheriff, when forced to arrest Vaughan for some infraction, simply waited until he sobered up, in which case he came along peaceably. But Vaughan could also be civic-minded in his own violent way. Jim Blakely, the sheriff who had helped rid the Crooked River country of its vigilantes in the early 1880s, had counted Hank Vaughan as his best friend and ally during those times, even while acknowledging that "he's been called a lot of hard names by the history writers."

In another episode in 1883, Vaughan was aboard a Northern Pacific Railroad train running between Oregon and Idaho when several robbers burst into the passenger car and demanded the travelers' valuables. Vaughan drew his revolver and began shooting, killing one of the bandits and driving the others off. For this bit of civic contribution, the Northern Pacific Railroad line supposedly presented him with a lifetime rail pass.

Sometime in the early 1880s, although still married to his first wife, Vaughan married Martha Robie, a Native-American woman who had rights to some fertile land on the Umatilla Indian Reservation east of Pendleton. It was also said that she had an inheritance of fifty thousand to seventy thousand dollars from her first husband. When his first wife, Lois, heard about Martha, she demanded a divorce, which Vaughan gave her.

Between the land on the reservation and his new wife's money, Vaughan set himself up in 1883 with a 640-acre wheat ranch that was apparently very successful. Given Vaughan's basic nature, he also continued his semi-legal horse-trading operations.

For a man who spent so much of his career trading lead with adversaries, the end came for Hank Vaughan in a surprising manner. One day in early June 1893, he mounted his horse—dressed in chaps and a little drunk—and galloped wildly down the main street of Pendleton while pedestrians looked on. Reaching a cross street, Vaughan turned his horse too suddenly and the animal stumbled, catapulting its rider out of the saddle and slamming him to the ground.

Bleeding and severely injured, he was carried off for treatment, reportedly saying to his rescuers, "It's pretty hard to kill me off." But his internal injuries were mortal, and he lingered until the morning of June 15, 1893. When he died, one of the last of the old-time gunfighters, his body was scarred with thirteen old bullet wounds. He was buried in the Olney Cemetery outside of Pendleton.

Incident at Chinese Massacre Cove
A Brutal Mass Murder

One hot sunny day in June of 1887, Wallowa County rancher George Craig and his son were riding along the Snake River on the Oregon–Idaho border. Perhaps looking for stray cattle, the two men found themselves in the vicinity of Dug Bar, a traditional Indian river crossing location downstream from the mouth of Deep Creek. This is a stretch of the river aptly called Hells Canyon. Something along the water's edge caught their eye—a glint of bones, half buried in mud and water.

The white, scattered bones of cattle and big game animals are a common sight in this country, so the two men probably did not think much of it. But when they approached more closely they discovered, to their horror, the relatively fresh skeletal remains of three or four human beings. The bodies had been so thoroughly worked over by wild animals that the two cowboys could not tell who they were or how they had died. They had obviously died somewhere else and floated downstream. Surveying the grisly scene, the Craigs wondered how this many men could die without it being talked about. When word finally did get around, it would be revealed that there were many more dead men lying in the still canyon.

The inspiration for naming this great breach in the earth's surface Hells Canyon did not come from this event—but it all too well describes what happened in late May 1887 when a gang of white men attacked two mining camps and killed as many

Hells Canyon, Wallowa County.
Jim Yuskavitch

as thirty-one Chinese miners, hacking their bodies to pieces. It was a brutal mass murder that would be largely forgotten for the next seventy years, until a county clerk discovered a stack of old court records in a long-forgotten safe.

Chinese workers were a common sight on the Oregon frontier. They began immigrating to the state in the mid-1850s, usually by way of California, to work in fish canneries and gold mining camps, on railroad construction crews, and at other jobs, often sending the money they earned to relatives back home in China.

By the 1860s, many Chinese workers had moved into the Oregon interior, especially to the Blue and Wallowa Mountains country where gold had been discovered. These immigrants typically worked for large mining companies or struck out on their own, searching for gold in less desirable locations or reworking the tailings that white miners had already searched, taking bits of previously overlooked gold. Through diligence and hard work, the Chinese miners were often able to wrest respectable amounts of gold from stream gravel that their white counterparts had considered played out.

Despite their contribution to the labor market and to local economies, Chinese miners were subject to considerable prejudice by whites. In the rowdy mining camps, the Chinese were commonly harassed, bullied, and sometimes much worse. Discrimination was all but official. In 1882 Congress passed the

Chinese Placer Miners.
Grant County Historical Museum

Chinese Exclusion Act, which established a ten-year moratorium on Chinese immigration into the United States. Chinese immigrants were also forbidden by law from becoming US citizens. Oregon law required resident Chinese to pay special fees and taxes that were not applicable to whites. County sheriffs often ignored crimes committed against Chinese workers in their jurisdictions. In 1885 arsonists burned down the Canyon City, Oregon, Chinatown. When city fathers refused to allow it to be rebuilt, the local Chinese community was forced to relocate to nearby John Day.

By the 1880s, the placer mines in northeast Oregon were beginning to run dry and white miners were moving on. Since the Chinese specialized in working played-out tailings, by the last two decades of the nineteenth century the majority of Oregon gold miners were Chinese. One of the places where they patiently and persistently washed and rewashed stream gravel, eyes looking sharp for glints of bright yellow, was on the floor of Hells Canyon.

Along with the miners, the rugged and remote Hells Canyon attracted outlaws of every stripe, especially horse thieves for whom the place was an effective refuge. It was a fateful meeting of these two groups that would trigger the Chinese Massacre of 1887.

Because of conflicting court depositions, deathbed confessions, and the reticence of old-timers, it is unlikely the exact details will ever be truly known. But enough information has come to light to give a general picture of what happened over that two-day period during the last week of May 1887.

What is known is that in late May of that year seven men— Robert McMillan, Hiram Maynard, Homer LaRue, Bruce Evans, Carl Hughes, Frank Vaughan, and T. J. "Tigh" Canfield, horse thieves all—were staying at a cabin at Dug Bar.

They were aware that upstream in Robinson Gulch, one-half mile down from Deep Creek, a camp of Chinese gold miners were working old tailings on behalf of a San Francisco–based Chinese mining company. The criminals knew that the Chinese had a knack for teasing out a little more gold from gravel that other miners had written off as barren, and the camp was likely to have a good amount of the precious ore in stock. Stealing gold from Chinese miners had to be easier and more lucrative than trading in stolen horses. They hatched a foul plan.

The accounts believed to be the most accurate say that, on the appointed day, Frank Vaughan stayed at the cabin while the other six filed out the door and made their way to Robinson Gulch.

There were ten miners working this camp. The six killers probably watched for a while as the miners went about their daily tasks. Then they started shooting. There must have been a brief moment of shock and disbelief as the first shot was fired. Chinese miners were used to being bullied, harassed, and treated unfairly, but this was obviously a premeditated assault. The shock must have turned to terror as the miners realized what was happening.

Exactly what took place during the relatively short time is not recorded. Did the miners have any weapons in camp that they might have used to defend themselves or did they attempt to flee for their lives? Whichever action they took, it was to no avail. When the horse thieves' guns fell silent, every miner in camp lay dead. But the criminals weren't done with their atrocities.

They first ransacked the camp looking for the miners' gold. No one knows how much, if any, they got. Guesses range from four thousand to more than fifty thousand dollars' worth. In a deathbed statement, one of the accused murderers would claim they took $50,500 in gold.

Placer Gold Mine.
Grant County Historical Museum

But then they unaccountably mutilated the bodies of their victims with knives and hatchets, pitching their remains into the river. With that brutal task completed, they returned to the cabin, where Vaughan was fixing their dinner.

Whether they decided there might be more gold back at the Robinson Gulch camp that they had missed or if they feared having left a witness alive, we'll never know. But the next morning, LaRue, Evans, and Canfield made a second trip to the camp. When they arrived they found eight more Chinese miners who had come downriver by boat to join their fellows, finding instead the sickening scene of death. The three murderers killed and mutilated these men as well, taking the miners' boat and floating it down the Snake River.

They drifted about four miles until they came to China Bar, the site of another gold mining camp operated by thirteen Chinese miners. Within minutes of the killers' arrival, all thirteen of these miners were dead too, their bodies hacked to pieces and thrown in the river to drift away. After searching this camp for gold, the three men returned to the cabin. Eventually the gang moved on.

A month later, another group of Chinese miners discovered the slaughter at the Robinson Gulch camp and reported it to the authorities in Lewiston, Idaho. At about the time that George Craig was finding the skeletons, more bodies were floating ashore at Lewiston some fifty miles away. Bodies reportedly turned up for years afterward.

Despite a long-held prejudice against the Chinese, the mass murder of thirty-one, and perhaps as many as thirty-four, miners prompted a great deal of shock among Wallowa County residents. The Chinese Consul and the Chinese Six Companies in San Francisco initiated an investigation into the murders. A federal investigator named F. K. Vincent from Lewiston was retained to conduct the investigation. The company and Chinese government also offered a one thousand dollar reward for the killers.

Vincent, who said that this crime was "the most cold-blooded, cowardly treachery" he had ever heard of, worked in the canyon trying to dig up leads. But it was slow going and dangerous work. He was watched with suspicion by the canyon residents and got little cooperation. Eventually, he came up with a list of suspects but not enough evidence to arrest them. One of those suspects was Frank Vaughan, whom Vincent tried to convince to turn state's evidence. Vaughan finally agreed and fingered his fellow gang members.

On March 23, 1888, a grand jury indicted Robert McMillan, Hiram Maynard, Homer LaRue, Bruce Evans, Carl Hughes, and Tigh Canfield on ten counts of murder. The dead men's names were listed as Ah Jim, Heop Gee, Hee Yee, La Bate, Hop Sing, Ye Lee, Wy See, Hee Lee, Sing Heim, and Heim Lim. It's questionable if these were their real names.

Gang members Bruce Evans, T. J. Canfield, and Carl Hughes had skedaddled from the area, but McMillan, Maynard, and LaRue were arrested in the spring of 1888 and thrown in jail to await trial. All three of their depositions, as well as Vaughan's, blamed the murders on Evans, Canfield, and Hughes, and claimed that the four of them had no prior knowledge of the plan and were afraid to try and stop it once the shooting started.

Even though the citizens of Wallowa County condemned the murders, thirty-three people signed a petition demanding that the three accused men be released on bail. Bail was granted for eight hundred dollars each.

The trial was held in late August 1888. No transcripts of the proceedings seemed to have survived, so the details of testimony are sketchy at best. But by any measure the conclusion was somewhat irregular and curious. The records show that the jury found McMillan, Maynard, and LaRue guilty of the murders. Then a strange thing happened, although the specifics are not known. After the verdict was announced, the jury apparently heard more testimony of an unknown nature. The judge then gave the jury additional instructions and sent them back for further deliberations. When they returned, the verdict had been changed to not guilty and the three defendants went free.

Evans, Canfield, and Hughes were never brought to trial for the murders, but rumors of their doings after the massacre have been passed along over the years. At one point Evans was arrested in Wallowa County for stealing horses but escaped before trial with the help of a pistol supplied by an unknown accomplice. It is believed he went to Montana, where his ultimate fate is unknown. LaRue drifted down to California where he was probably killed in a card-game dispute. Canfield eventually moved to Idaho to work as a blacksmith after spending some time in the Kansas State Penitentiary.

As for justice, the thirty-one massacred miners would have none. The few weeks that McMillan, Maynard, and LaRue spent in jail waiting for trial were the only punishment anyone received for the crime. In 1889 the US government paid the Chinese government nearly $277,000 as "full indemnity" for the massacre, although it is extremely doubtful any of the miners' family members saw a penny of it.

These many decades later, nothing can be done for the murdered men. But in October 2005 the site of the former mining camp just below Deep Creek was officially named Chinese Massacre Cove by the US Board on Geographical Names and the Oregon Geographical Names Board. In June 2012 a granite memorial was placed at Chinese Massacre Cove, inscribed with the words: CHINESE MASSACRE COVE. SITE OF THE 1887 MASSACRE OF AS MANY AS 34 CHINESE GOLD MINERS. NO ONE WAS HELD ACCOUNTABLE. At the very least, no one now will forget the murderous events that happened there.

Carl Panzram

A Budding Serial Killer Comes to Oregon

The crime of murder has been as common in Oregon as it has been everywhere else, and for all of the same reasons. Revenge, passion, anger, and money are all motives for this most heinous of crimes, and the state of Oregon has seen its share.

Simple greed is often the prime driver for murder because a dead robbery victim can neither resist the thief nor report the crime to police. But the enterprise seldom ends well for the murderer. Take, for example, the murder of forty-two-year-old Boise, Idaho, sheep buyer R. C. Goodwin, whose body, clothed only in underwear, was found in the Snake River in Malheur County, Oregon, in September 1916.

The victim was suspected of being from out of the area, since the investigating officers, Sheriff Ben J. Brown and Deputy Sheriff Lee Noe, didn't recognize him and he carried no identification. But there was a clue—the laundry number found inside his underwear. A check with commercial laundries in Boise, the nearest city with laundries that used a numbering system, eventually matched his identity and located his residence at the Manitou Hotel in that frontier city.

Brown and Noe considered potential motives, including a business rival or other enemy, or perhaps a jealous former boyfriend of the deceased's fiancée, a local Boise woman. But a little more detective work found that he had come to Ontario, Oregon, to buy sheep and had visited a number of area ranches looking for stock to purchase. A buyer of livestock was likely to be carrying a lot of cash as well as a checkbook, and traveling alone through the remote reaches of Oregon's ranch country would leave such a person vulnerable to foul play. Now the case pointed to robbery as the motive.

The sheriff and his deputy questioned a number of suspects, but they couldn't link any of them to the crime. But the investigators weren't beat yet. The bullet that killed Goodwin was from a .38 caliber handgun and a check of the local hardware stores found that a handyman named Dave Brichoux had recently purchased a great deal of such ammunition. Further investigations found that Brichoux had also recently been in Winnemucca, Nevada, where he had cashed one of Goodwin's checks for five hundred dollars at a local bank, presenting the teller with the dead man's identification and claiming to be him.

With that evidence brought against him, Brichoux confessed. When brought to trial, he was found guilty and sentenced on October 27, 1911, to life in prison at the Oregon State Penitentiary. But he was released in 1927 and three months later murdered the wife of a physician during the course of an extortion scheme. Sentenced again to prison, he committed suicide there in 1933.

Passion is a reason for murder as old as love itself. Consider the case of Charity Lamb, the wife of a Willamette Valley homesteader who, in 1854, was brought to trial for the axe murder of her husband Nathaniel Lamb, whom she crept upon from behind and whacked on the head twice before running off, leaving him to die in a pool of blood.

Quickly captured and brought to trial, the Charity Lamb affair became one of Oregon's earliest scandals as the facts came forward under the testimony of various witnesses and the story of a love triangle among Charity, her daughter Mary Ann, and an itinerant laborer named Collins unfolded.

Collins had shown up in the Willamette Valley in the summer of 1853, six years before Oregon would become a state, and took odd jobs near the Lamb homestead. Charity Lamb and Collins eventually met and she quickly became enamored of him, as did her daughter. But Collins had other plans that included a move to California, and Lamb, unable to bear his going away, promised to follow after him and bring Mary Ann along as well.

First she had to get rid of her husband. But as she swung the axe that split Nathaniel's skull, Collins was long gone and his affairs with her and Mary Ann were a distant, and unimportant, memory.

The trial was a spectacle and heavily covered—and sensationalized—by the newspapers. Under the weight of damning testimony by her son, along with the doctors who examined her husband's body, she was quickly convicted, despite her lawyers' attempts to paint her as an abused wife who killed in self-defense. Charity Lamb spent the rest of her days in prison as Oregon's first convicted female murderer.

But serial murder is something else altogether, terrifying to the public because it is random, without reason or apparent cause, and therefore difficult for the police to solve.

One of the earliest Oregon cases of serial killing happened in Benton County in the Willamette Valley, a region settled by farmers who traveled the Oregon Trail by covered wagon beginning in the 1840s.

The body of Eliza A. Griffin was found on June 2, 1910, and the Benton County Sheriff's Department could not determine if the cause of death was murder or suicide. But nearly a year later George Humphrey, a Benton County resident, confessed to the murder. Then, his brother Charles confessed to helping George commit the crime. But more shocking than the confession for the Griffin murder was Charles's testimony that George had killed three people the previous year, including George Selby near Dallas, George Damrose of Hayhurst Valley, and George's father-in-law, William King. That same year George Humphrey attempted to murder Ole Olson in the town of Yoncalla in July 1910. Charles also implicated his brother in the disappearance of Dallas resident Newton I. Patterson in the summer of 1903.

But the most sinister serial killer ever to cross over the state line into Oregon—and possibly one of the most notorious murderers in US history—was Carl Panzram, whose rage and anger at the world and life itself, so he claimed, drove him to murder twenty-one human beings and horribly abuse many more.

In mid-April of 1915, Carl Panzram drifted into Astoria, Oregon. He had hopped a freight train in Montana, where he had just completed a one-year sentence at the prison in Deer Lodge for burglary. Upon his release, he was presented with a new suit and five bucks to begin a new life. But Panzram had in mind continuing his old one.

He picked the right place. Astoria, on the northernmost tip of the Oregon coast where the Columbia River empties into the sea, was one of the toughest port towns in the US at the turn of the nineteenth century, and was known especially for its trade in shanghaiing unwary sailors and shipping them off against their will for years of servitude aboard some of the most scurvy ships commanded by the cruelest captains that ever sailed the seas.

Panzram was without a doubt right at home in such a place. Arriving in Astoria at twenty-three years of age, he was muscle-bound and had already spent years in prison, mostly for burglary and petty larceny. He was not yet a killer, but his criminal tenure in Oregon would give him his first taste of murder as a player in the demise of a high-level government official. After that, there was no keeping Panzram from his criminal destiny.

Biographical accounts report that Carl Panzram was born to German parents, John and Lizzie Panzram—he from East Prussia, she from Berlin—on the family farm in northern Minnesota on June 28, 1891, although his Oregon State Penitentiary records record his "nativity" as Alabama.

By all accounts his childhood was a harsh one, and he, along with five brothers and one sister, toiled alongside his parents to scrape out a living. By the time Panzram was seven, his parents' marriage had crumbled under the weight of John Panzram's heavy drinking and reportedly violent personality. The divorce proceedings involved the elder Panzram, John, simply leaving home one day and never returning.

As young Carl grew older he evidently took on more and more of his father's traits and in 1903, at the age of twelve, he was taken from the farm and placed in the Minnesota State Training School in Red Wing, Minnesota, a reform school that housed about three hundred boys from ten to twenty years old. He was admitted on October 11, 1903.

Accounts vary as to the reason he was sent to reform school, where conditions may not have been all that much harsher than his home life. Some say that he became an unrepentant and chronic thief at an early age, brought on partly by beatings and other abusive behavior visited upon him by his brothers. Some of those early criminal exploits include burglary of a neighbor's home when he was eleven and theft of a firearm. Other accounts simply say he was incorrigible and a "holy terror."

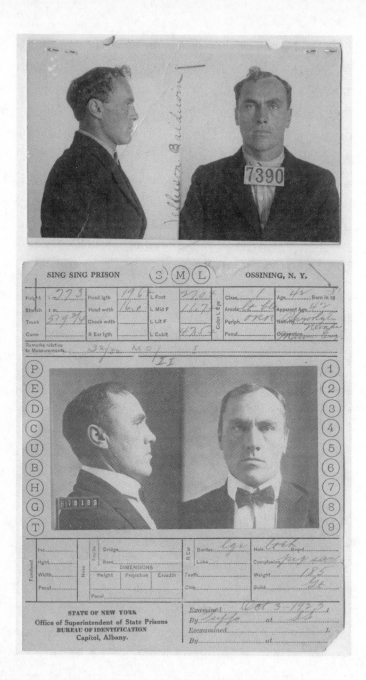

Carl Panzram's Oregon State Penitentiary and Sing Sing mug shots.
Oregon State Archives

Life at the Minnesota State Training School was apparently a routine of hard labor, formal education, and religious instruction, punctuated by frequent beatings and other corporal punishment that only served to make young Carl more sullen, angry, and rebellious. He managed to get a full serving of revenge by concocting a scheme to burn down the building that housed the school's paint shop. Wrapping a length of heavy cotton string around a stick, he lit one end and placed it out of sight in the building along with some oil-soaked rags. The building burned to the ground to the tune of one hundred thousand dollars in damages. School authorities never knew that he was the perpetrator of the fiery event and a few months later, near the end of 1905, Panzram was judged reformed enough to be released back to his mother's custody, although in later years Panzram claimed he earned his parole by simply telling the parole board what they wanted to hear.

Back home it didn't take long for everyone to see that the nearly two years spent in the reformatory had not improved his attitude or outlook on life. Always an angry, sullen boy, now he was even worse. By then, Lizzie Panzram had sold their homestead in Minnesota and had moved to a small rented house in Grand Forks, Michigan.

Young Panzram's life with his mother in their new home was made all the harder by the taunts of the other kids in the neighborhood who were well aware of where he had spent the previous couple of years. By late March 1906, fourteen-year-old Carl had enough of "family life" and hopped a freight train headed west out of East Grand Forks.

He rode the rails as a hobo throughout the Midwest for a time and along the way claimed that he was attacked and molested by a group of older men, an assault that added more fuel to the bonfire of rage that burned within him. Eventually, he ended up in Montana.

Once settled down in Big Sky country, it didn't take long for Panzram to get into trouble and soon he was serving a one-year sentence at the Montana State Reform School in Miles City for burglary. It was here that Panzram made his initial, although unsuccessful, attempt at murder, slamming a guard on the head with a piece of wood in retaliation for his constant "pestering."

The guard recovered. Panzram got a beating and came under even more scrutiny and pestering by his jailers. But he and another inmate managed to escape and the following year, in 1907, he enlisted in the US Army, and was subsequently court-martialed for theft while stationed at Fort William Henry Harrison in western Montana. He was sentenced to three years in Fort Leavenworth, Kansas, followed by a dishonorable discharge.

Released in 1910 after serving his entire sentence, Panzram kicked around Colorado and Mexico before ending up back in Montana and the prison at Deer Lodge, then on to Oregon.

By now a hardened career criminal, Panzram did, upon his arrival in Astoria, what all criminals are inclined to do—commit a crime. On June 1, 1915, Panzram, now going by the alias Jeff Baldwin, burglarized the Astoria home of C. R. Higgins, president of the Bank of Astoria. But within a few days, Panzram was arrested while trying to pawn some of the stolen property—which reportedly included silverware, table setting items, gold shirt studs, and items of clothing—at some of the local dives.

Caught red-handed with items that matched the description of the stolen property, Panzram, aka Jeff Baldwin, confessed to the crime. With a promise of leniency by county Sheriff J. V. Burns and District Attorney C. W. Mullins if he revealed where *handwritten:* 7390

$50
REWARD

Escaped from the Oregon State Penitentiary

JEFF BALDWIN

Description	Moles, Marks, Scars, Etc.
AGE when received, 27	Slanting scar on left side of head; horizontal scar under right side of mouth; pit scar under right cheek; scar on second joint of middle finger right hand.
HEIGHT, 5 feet 9 1-2 inches	
WEIGHT, 168 pounds	
COMPLEXION, medium	
HAIR, med. brown	
EYES, grey blue	
BUILD, heavy	Discarded clothing will bear the number 7390
NATIVITY, Alabama	
OCCUPATION, thief	
FINGER PRINT $\dfrac{32 \ \text{M} \ \text{O}}{32 \ \text{I} \ \text{I}}$	Formerly in Montana penitentiary

FIFTY ($50) DOLLARS REWARD WILL BE PAID BY THE WARDEN OF THE OREGON STATE PENITENTIARY FOR THE ARREST, DETENTION AND ADVICE OF THE ABOVE, WHO WAS RECEIVED AT THE PENITENTIARY June 24, 1915

Under sentence of 7 years from Clatsop county.
Charged with larceny in a dwelling
Escaped from Prison September 18, 1917

Anyone seeing above please phone or telegraph to the Warden, State Penitentiary, and charge to penitentiary. Phone 12.

Salem, Ore., Sept 18, 1917 CHAS. A. MURPHY, Warden

Carl Panzram's "Jeff Baldwin" wanted poster.

Oregon State Archives

he had hidden the rest of the loot, Panzram led them to where he had stashed his ill-gotten gains near the docks along the river.

While Panzram honored his part of the bargain, the judge who presided over his trial did not and sentenced him to seven years in prison. While waiting in the Astoria jail to be transferred to prison to serve his sentence, and furious over this perceived double-cross, he managed to get out of his cell, gather up furniture, papers, and other flammable material from the jail office and set the pile ablaze. Sheriff's deputies burst in and doused the flames before they could do any damage, then gave him a good beating for his effort. It was to be Oregon law enforcement authorities' first taste of Panzram's behavior when under lock and key.

Later that month—June 1915—he was shackled and transported by train to the Oregon State Penitentiary, where he was to become one of the most difficult and dangerous convicts ever to be incarcerated in that institution.

The Oregon State Penitentiary was the first state prison in the United States. Initially built in 1842 in Oregon City, it was called the Oregon Territorial Jail. But it burned down on August 18, 1846 and a new one was constructed in Portland in 1851. Inmates displaced by the Oregon City jail fire were housed in a former Portland whisky shop until the new prison was finished.

But chronic escapes and difficulties reaching road access agreements with the city of Portland eventually necessitated the need for a new prison, and in 1866 the penitentiary was moved to its present location east of Salem.

Even in the new facility escapes continued to be a regular activity for prisoners, leading the warden at the time, J. C. Gardner, to invent the notorious Gardner Shackle, more commonly known as the Oregon Boot. Developed in 1866, this device was a thick iron band fixed around an inmate's ankle that served to interfere with his balance that made running and other athletic maneuvers difficult and awkward. The Oregon Boot, although regarded as cruel by many, was effective in its objective and served to reduce the number of escapees from the prison.

Giving inmates jobs to keep them busy and aid in their rehabilitation was a cornerstone of Oregon's incarceration philosophy. The program was begun at the Portland institution with a brick-making machine that, in addition to giving the inmates something to do, also generated a revenue stream for the prison. More industrial ventures were added when the Salem facility opened, including a tannery, shoe and boot assembly, sawmill, and stove factory. In addition, inmates worked at various tasks involved in running the prison, including serving in the print shop, laundry room, butcher shop, officers' barber shop, creamery, and dining room, and landscaping the grounds. All prisoners were required to work. It was into this environment that Panzram, aka Jeff Baldwin, Inmate No. 7390, was processed.

His official description reads:

AGE when received, 27
HEIGHT, 5 feet 9 1/2 inches
WEIGHT, 168 pounds
COMPLEXION, medium
HAIR, med. brown
EYES, grey blue
BUILD, heavy
NATIVITY, Alabama
OCCUPATION, thief

Slanting scar on left side of head; horizontal
scar under right side of mouth; pit scar under
right cheek; scar on second joint of middle
finger right hand.

The prison superintendent at the time of Panzram's arrival was Harry Minto. Minto had been Salem chief of police from 1892 to 1896, and then served two terms as sheriff of Marion County. In 1914, when Minto was fifty-one years old, Governor James Withycombe appointed him as superintendent of the Oregon State Penitentiary.

Although by some accounts Warden Minto had the reputation of being a hard, even cruel, disciplinarian, what went on at the Oregon State Penitentiary was probably not uncommon for that time period in American penal history.

The Oregon Boot was regularly used and chain gangs were a standard form of both punishment and utilizing convict labor. The penalty for the unruly and troublemaking inmate included solitary confinement in the "dungeon" or "bull pen," where, according to (unconfirmed) rumors that circulated through the inmate population, prisoners were sometimes arbitrarily shot by guards who then made it look like an escape attempt. Whippings and beatings were not rare punishments, either. The day-to-day life of a prisoner in the Oregon State Penitentiary was strictly controlled. Inmates had rules and routines to which they were expected to adhere without question and woe to those who felt they were exempt.

Panzram was undeterred by authority, and not inclined to do anything he did not care to do. In fact, he was in trouble within a few days of his arrival, dumping his full "soil pan" onto a guard one morning, which earned him a beating and a thirty-day stint in solitary confinement. Back out in the general prisoner population, Panzram proved to be not only a trouble-maker, but an unsettling influence on his fellow inmates, who often avoided him for that reason.

Chafing from the many punishments he received for his regular acts of insubordination, Panzram would soon get the ultimate revenge on his nemesis and object of his hatred—Superintendent Harry Minto—through another inmate named Otto Hooker.

Panzram had been agitating Hooker—who had beat an earlier murder rap but was now serving time for burglary—to attempt an escape, advising him to request duty on one of the prison's chain gangs that would take him outside the penitentiary walls and offer an opportunity to slip away. Hooker surprised Panzram by not only taking his advice but also actually pulling off an escape, darting into the woods on the foggy morning of September 27, 1915, while the guards weren't paying attention.

Minto formed a posse in search of the escapee, which he personally led. The lawmen followed Hooker's trail in the direction of Jefferson, a small agricultural town about twenty miles south of Salem. One of them, Jefferson Marshal J. J. Benson, stumbled upon Hooker, who was still dressed in his prison garb, and the two struggled. Benson's gun went off, leaving him lying on the ground with a slug embedded near his collarbone. Hooker grabbed Benson's handgun and lit out.

Now Hooker was armed and dangerous, and the search for him intensified over the course of the day and evening. At 11:30 p.m., Harry Minto and Officer Walter Johnson were walking the railroad tracks two miles north of Albany when they heard someone approaching. Concealing themselves in the under-brush along the tracks, they waited. It was Hooker, and Minto leapt onto the tracks, pistol drawn. But Hooker was faster and put a single bullet into the superintendent's head. Minto fell to the ground dead. Johnson blazed away with his sidearm, but Hooker beat an escape unscathed.

Inflamed by Minto's murder, more officers were enlisted in the chase and by the early morning hours they found him holed up in an abandoned house in Albany. Hooker feigned surrender then pulled his gun. But this time the lawmen were ready and Patrolman A. J. Long shot him. Seriously wounded, Hooker was rushed to St. Mary's Hospital in an attempt to save his life, but he died at 2:05 a.m.

It's not likely that Panzram mourned either Minto's or Hooker's passing. Whatever his thoughts on those matters, or his crucial accessory role in Harry Minto's murder, Panzram continued to cause trouble regularly for the superintendents who replaced him, including earning a couple of months in the "hole" for trying to burn down the prison flax mill, one of the prison's money-making enterprises, in May 1916.

The following year, on September 18, Panzram finally managed to slip away, hiding in the nearby woods for a time, then stealing a bicycle to put more distance between himself and the prison. A wanted poster went out offering fifty dollars for information leading to the capture of Jeff Baldwin.

On the loose for about a week, Panzram burgled a house, stealing a gun, then got into a gunfight with a local deputy sheriff who recognized him. Panzram was captured, and after an unsuccessful struggle to escape from the police car, was transported back to the penitentiary.

Tried for the burglary and attempted murder of the sheriff's deputy, Panzram got ten years, which, when added to the time remaining on his original sentence, totaled fourteen years.

But he would not serve that time in Oregon. On May 12, 1918, Panzram sawed through the bars of one of the prison windows, lowered himself to the ground, and made for the woods under a hail of gunfire from guards on the wall, then vanished from rifle range and from sight. Panzram took the alias John O'Leary and hopped an eastbound freight train, never to return to Oregon.

Two years later, Panzram committed his first murders— ten sailors along the New York City waterfront. He killed two small boys in New England in 1922 and by the time he was arrested for burglary in Washington, D.C., in 1928, he claimed to have murdered twenty-one people—some during the course of robberies but many apparently just for the sake of the killing.

Ironically, Panzram was never arrested or tried for any of the murders to which he admitted. His 1928 sentence of twenty-five years in Leavenworth Federal Penitentiary was for his long record of burglary and similar property crimes. What finally brought Panzram to the gallows on September 5, 1930, was his bludgeoning to death of prison laundry foreman Robert Warnke the year before, after Warnke discovered one of Panzram's prison scams and threatened to expose him.

The state of Oregon unsuccessfully attempted to have him returned to complete his sentence at the Oregon State Penitentiary, and his Oregon State inmate file, at about 120 pages, is considerably longer than average. But on his day in court in 1917 as Jeff Baldwin, Carl Panzram swore that he would never serve his fourteen-year Oregon sentence. That was a vow the serial-killer-to-be was able to keep.

The Triskett Gang
Shootout At Sailors' Diggings

Surrounded, the defenders fired down on their pursuers from atop a small hill near the southwestern Oregon frontier town of O'Brien. It was a short but fierce battle. Weighed down by stolen gold, the thieves attempted a desperate escape as the posse that followed after them slowly closed the distance. After fleeing less than half a dozen miles, the five horsemen were finally forced to seek the high ground in a last-ditch effort to save themselves. But the men were hopelessly outnumbered and outgunned, and when the shooting was over, four members of the Triskett Gang were dead, and the fifth lay dying.

Violence was not an uncommon occurrence in the gold mining country and camps of Josephine County in the 1850s, but what the Triskett Gang had done on that summer day in 1852, in a place called Sailors' Diggings, was beyond the pale and accounted for the swiftness of the justice visited upon them and how mercilessly it was applied. And the crime for which they paid so dearly wasn't the theft of gold.

Everyone knows the story of the great California gold rush, when, in 1848, John Sutter, who ran a sawmill near Sacramento, discovered gold in his mill's tailrace. Word got out about the discovery at Sutter's Mill, and beginning in 1849 thousands of people made a beeline to California seeking their fortunes in the gold fields. A few would become rich. Most would be disappointed.

In the sweep of American history, that discovery was no small thing. It brought a new rush of settlers to the West, just as the great migration of settlers to Oregon's Willamette Valley via the Oregon Trail in search of fertile farmland had done beginning a few years earlier.

Discovery of gold in California and later in other parts of the West also significantly increased the world's gold supply. Between 1841 and 1850 the world's gold mines produced 6,522,913 fine ounces of the precious metal. In the following decade, the worldwide production of gold increased by 270 percent, primarily due to the gold discoveries in the western United States.

By 1850, some California miners began to move north to southern Oregon into what are now Josephine and Jackson Counties to explore for gold, since the terrain and geology of that region was similar to that of the northern California gold fields.

And find gold they did, in 1851 at Jackson and Canyon Creeks, and then at Sailors' Diggings. Those discoveries had the same effect on the settlers in the Willamette Valley as the find at Sutter's Mill had on speculators and adventurers from other regions of the country, and soon hundreds of Oregon farmers traded in their mules and plows for shovels and gold pans, and headed south to make their fortune—although most gave up soon after arriving and went back to the less glamorous but more economically stable occupation of farming.

However, many miners did stay—perhaps one thousand white and Chinese settlers in Josephine County in the early 1850s, not counting the indigenous people. Their presence created demand for products and services that resulted in the establishment of various businesses to serve the miners, and many mining camps evolved into small towns.

But the history of Sailors' Diggings was a little different. The story goes that in 1851 a party of sailors, who upon hearing rumors of gold in southern Oregon decided to change careers, jumped ship at some West Coast port, San Francisco, perhaps, and made their way north to the headwaters of the Illinois River in the Siskiyou Mountains. After digging around for a time, they finally found gold in a gulch they called Sailor Gulch. Eventually, a twenty- to twenty-five-square-mile or so area around Sailor Gulch came to be called Sailors' Diggings. This area included Frye, Taylor, Shelly Butcher, Caro, and Waldo Gulches. Eventually the small settlements of Takilma and O'Brien were included as well. Nevertheless, the largest settlement in the Josephine County gold mining area at that time was Waldo, and references to Sailors' Diggings and Waldo were often interchangeable.

Mining for gold in Josephine County, and southwestern Oregon in general, proved quite lucrative and, excepting a brief period in the 1850s when mining activities were interrupted by the Rogue River Indian War, the miners kept themselves quite busy on their claims. Reliable figures on how much gold was taken out of the ground and streams in the Sailors' Diggings area during these early years are elusive, but records show that Oregon produced $8 to $20 million worth of gold in 1866, and there is little doubt that a significant percentage of the state's net worth in gold came from its remote southwestern mountains.

A number of technologies had been developed for teasing gold out of the earth and rivers, and when miners first arrived in the Sailors' Diggings region they used the tried and true method of placer mining. Although tedious and not especially efficient, placer mining was a simple and inexpensive way to transfer the coveted ore from the ground into a miner's purse.

At its most basic level, a miner used a pan in which he scooped up water and gravel from a riverbed, then carefully swished it around, letting some water and lighter dirt and gravel wash out over the rim, leaving the heavier material, such as gold, in the pan. A more efficient variation was a rocker, which utilized a wooden box and riffled bottom or screened mesh. The miner shoveled dirt and gravel from the streambed into the box then added water as he rocked the box back and forth to separate the lighter gravel from the heavier gold. A larger version of the rocker was a Long Tom, which was operated by several miners, and a sluice box was a longer version of a Long Tom that could be many hundreds of feet long with water permanently redirected from a stream to wash the gold out of the gravel and flush it to a location where it was collected. This method was an industrial mining technique and beyond the means of the individual miner. By the 1870s, after the more easily accessible gold had been found, mining companies went with more efficient, large-scale mining methods such as hydraulic mining. But in the 1850s, the miners of Sailors' Diggings spent their days placer mining, hoping that either this day or the next would make them wealthy men.

This rough country attracted equally rough men, and trouble was a regular part of life in the gold fields. A major threat to the miners as they poured into southern Oregon from California in the 1850s was the local Indian tribes. In addition to invading the territory of the various indigenous people, mining activity did considerable destruction to the environment upon which the Indians depended for their survival. The fact that the miners and other settlers treated the Indians brutally didn't help matters, and a war broke out during that decade known as the Rogue River Indian War, after the tribes that inhabited the Rogue River region.

Although the Indian resistance was eventually crushed, the miners around Sailors' Diggings took hits as well. In one instance, in mid-October 1855, a Mr. Jackson discovered the bodies of a Mr. Wilson and Mr. Hudson, packers who were driving a mule team pulling wagons loaded with merchandise over the Siskiyou Mountains from Crescent City, California. Their bodies were pierced with multiple arrows and their goods strewn along the road. A few weeks later, another wagon train near Sailors' Diggings was attacked—one packer killed, one wounded, and two missing, the merchandise stolen and the wagons pushed off a cliff.

With so much valuable gold around, thievery was a constant threat, especially from stagecoach robbers, known as "road agents." The bandits' favorite and most lucrative targets were the stagecoaches that carried gold from the southern Oregon gold field to banks in Sacramento and Portland via lonely mountain roads. A single gold shipment could be worth as much as ten thousand dollars, making a single successful heist well worth the risk. The road agents would hide in the timber and brush along the road and then leap out in front of the oncoming stage, brandishing a shotgun or rifle and ordering the driver to toss the express box, which held the gold, to the ground. Robberies were often staged at night; however, bolder bandits operated in the daytime as well. The pickings were so good that the one of the most celebrated road agents of the period, Charles "Black Bart" Boles, even made a special trip up from California to rob stagecoaches in the Siskiyous.

Gunfights and shootings erupted in the southern Oregon mining country from time to time as well. In the late 1850s, Sailors' Diggings packer Sam Brannan regularly drove a pack train over the Siskiyou Mountains to Crescent City and Happy

Waldo (Sailors' Diggings).
Josephine County Historical Society

Camp in northern California, returning with goods needed by the Oregon miners. On one trip he happened upon a fellow packer on the road to California, a packer who owed Brannan some money and had been in no hurry to pay him back.

Brannan demanded what was owed, but laughter was the only payoff he got. Angered, Brannan drew his knife. The other man drew a pistol and shot his creditor dead on the spot.

Frontier justice could be swift and merciless, but it could also be practical. Brannan's assailant was hauled off to trial in Sailors' Diggings on a charge of murder and acquitted on the grounds of self-defense.

But Sailors' Diggings could be just as dangerous as the surrounding wild mountains and lonely stagecoach roads, especially with outlaws like Boone Helm and Ferd Patterson wandering the streets.

When Boone Helm rode into town in the early 1860s, he was already an accomplished outlaw with robbery and murder as his specialties. Helm did his first killing in Missouri, stabbing an acquaintance to death in 1851, and then fled to the gold fields of California and San Francisco. After killing at least three men in California, he made his way to Oregon, ending up at The Dalles on the Columbia River where he got himself arrested over some minor scrapes with the law. He managed to escape, and lit out for Utah. Over the next several years he showed up in California; back to The Dalles, Canada; then Olympia, Washington, where he was arrested, but again escaped. By then he had murdered at least eight more men, but always managed to get away whenever he was captured.

He drifted into Sailors' Diggings around 1863, and was taken in by a local farmer who was unaware of Helm's criminal background. After accepting the farmer's kindness and charity for several weeks, Helm pretended to take his leave, really planning to return to murder his benefactor and rustle his herd of cattle. But an acquaintance of Helm's warned the farmer of the plot, and when Helm came back he was directed to continue on his way by the barrel of the farmer's shotgun.

Helm met his end in 1864 in Idaho Territory, where, as a member of the Henry Plummer gang, notorious road agents, he was captured and hanged in Virginia City on January 14.

Ferd Patterson, on the other hand, was a gunfighter in the true fashion of the old Wild West. Attired in a long black coat, vest, plaid pants, and a wide-brimmed cowboy hat, he looked the part. The lethal component of his outfit consisted of an ivory-handled Colt .31 caliber revolver and matching Bowie knife that usually got him out of whatever trouble he got himself into.

After a history of scrapes with the law and shootouts in the California gold camps and in San Francisco, Patterson wandered into Sailors' Diggings in 1859 and circulated throughout the saloons in the area plying his other profession—gambling at the card tables. The miners were no match for Patterson's skills and readily gave up their gold to him.

But it wasn't long before he managed to get on the bad side of George Wells, the local lawman and former Texas Ranger, although the reason for their mutual animosity is unclear. Eventually, it would have to come to a head, and it did one afternoon in front of a saloon in Sailors' Diggings, although by this time the town was called Waldo. An argument of unknown origin broke out between the two men, hard words were shouted, and then revolvers were drawn and gunfire echoed through town. A slug from Wells's .44 Walker Colt revolver slammed into Patterson's side, and he went down, shooting as he fell. Bullets from Patterson's ivory-handled pistol shattered one of Wells's arms. Then the fight was over as swiftly as it had begun. Both men recovered from their wounds, although Wells ended up with a permanently disabled arm.

Curiously, Patterson was not charged with any crime, despite the fact that he had fired on, and attempted to kill, an officer of the law. Once he was able to travel, the gunfighter returned to California, moseyed back up to Oregon, over to Idaho next, and then to Washington. But he continued his habit of getting on the bad side of people and in February 1866 a resentful rival with a grudge gunned Patterson down as he walked out of a Walla Walla, Washington, barbershop.

The origins of the Triskett Gang are murky. What is known is that the gang was named after the brothers Henry and Jack Triskett, and their three accomplices, Chris Stover, Fred Cooper, and Miles Hearn, filled out the rest of the membership. Why, exactly, they were in Sailors' Diggings on the afternoon of August 3, 1852, isn't known for certain. The outlaws hailed from

California where they apparently specialized in robbing miners on the California gold fields, which included murder when necessary to accomplish their aims. Most accounts say that they were running from a California posse after a string of robberies and dashed into southern Oregon hoping to give them the slip in its rugged mountains and scattered mining towns and camps. But in 1852, the southern Oregon gold fields were producing a lot of the precious metal and the gang members very well may have made their way to Sailors' Diggings with the idea of seeing how much of that gold they could mine for themselves, but with six-shooters rather than gold pans.

It would be a few more years before Sailors' Diggings would be more commonly called Waldo, and for a short time the seat of Josephine County. When the Triskett Gang came to town it still bore its original name and was fairly well developed, including a blacksmith shop, cobbler shop, butcher shop, some dry good stores, and several hotels and saloons. It was one of the latter to which the Triskett Gang paid a visit.

The five outlaws spent a good part of the afternoon in the saloon, drinking and becoming increasingly inebriated. Eventually, feeling restless or perhaps bored, Fred Cooper got up from his chair and staggered through the saloon door and onto the street. Then, without a word or any indication of what he was about to do next, Cooper pulled his revolver from its holster and shot a passerby dead. Hearing the shot, the rest of the gang jumped up and burst outside to see what the ruckus was all about. One look at the former Sailors' Diggings resident sprawled on the ground, and the gang's murderous instincts were instantly ignited.

The killing spree had begun. Revolvers drawn, the five outlaws began firing randomly at anybody unfortunate enough to be taking an afternoon walk down the main drag of Sailors' Diggings. Anyone

Miners panning for gold in a Josephine County, Oregon, stream.
Josephine County Historical Society

was a suitable target—men, women, and even a few children. What caused the shooting spree? Panic, perhaps? There is no way to know. But in a few minutes sixteen more bodies lay on the street.

Being miners, most of the town's menfolk were in the surrounding hills and gulches working their claims as the carnage transpired. But the old-fashioned black powder cap-and-ball pistols the gang used would have produced a terrible din and a great cloud of gray smoke and the miners would have heard, and in some cases seen, that some terrible event was taking place in town. From all over the surrounding area, the miners dropped their gold pans and shovels, grabbed their rifles, mounted their horses, and made for Sailors' Diggings in a hurry.

Back in town, the Triskett Gang knew that their time was short, and that armed and angry miners would soon come to the rescue of the townsfolk. The gang had one last order of business

Hydraulic gold mining, Josephine County, Oregon.
Josephine County Historical Society

to take care of before hightailing it—a trip to the Sailors' Diggings assayer's office. Rushing into the office with guns drawn, they took all the gold on hand then made the assayer their murder victim number eighteen. They also left two women on the street, alive but assaulted, bruised, and beaten.

Now their time was up, and they had to skedaddle. In the hope of giving their soon-to-be pursuers the slip, the gang might have considered going cross-country. But bushwhacking through the rugged and heavily vegetated terrain would probably have been too slow going. In addition, they were carrying a lot of stolen gold. Their haul from the Sailors' Diggings assay office has been estimated at between $25,000 and $75,000 worth of the precious rocks, and may have weighed up to 250 pounds. Some accounts of the massacre say they "borrowed" two packhorses to carry their stolen cargo, but even if they did, that additional weight would have slowed their escape considerably.

More than likely, the gang took the old Waldo Road west toward the mining camp of O'Brien, about six or seven miles away. That route would have taken them parallel to Fry Gulch, then south on the road to O'Brien.

But they didn't make it that far. Just a mile or two east of the mining camp, with the posse of vengeful miners now in sight and numbering many times more than they, the Trisketts and company made for the summit of a low hill and hunkered down for a shootout.

The fight didn't last long. Seeing the outlaws whip their horses up the hill, the miners quickly surrounded it, positioning themselves behind trees, stumps, and rocks. Then they began firing, sending fierce volleys of slugs into the outlaws' position. The Triskett Gang was doomed and it was over in a few minutes. The Triskett brothers, along with Fred Cooper and Miles Hearn, were dead. Chris Stover was still alive, although seriously wounded. The miners slung him up on a horse and brought him back to Sailors' Diggings for a proper hanging, but he died too soon.

The fight was over, and justice had been meted out to the Triskett Gang. All that was left for the miners to do was bury the dead and go back to their claims.

But there is a twist to the story. The gold that the gang lifted from the assayer wasn't with the outlaws or their effects when the miners searched the hilltop in the battle's aftermath. Despite continued searches afterward, the gold was never located, leading to speculation that the gang buried the gold either on the hill where they made their last stand or somewhere along the road as they fled, and a legend has grown over the years of the lost treasure of the Triskett Gang. Occasionally some modern-day treasure seeker ventures into the hills around O'Brien in search of the hidden gold, worth millions today. But to date no one has yet struck this mother lode.

As for Sailors' Diggings, it, like the Triskett Gang, has faded into history. Eventually renamed Waldo, and for a time an important community in Josephine County, its fortunes faded as the gold eventually played out and it became a ghost town. In the 1930s, a gravel mining company purchased the town site and took out the gravel for building material, destroying the last of the old buildings in the process. Today, all that is left of the former Sailors' Diggings–Waldo is, perhaps appropriately, an old graveyard.

Bibliography

Alexander, Doug. "Secret Deal." *The Beaver*, Canada's National History Society, December/January 2006, pp. 22–27.

Anderson, Frank W. *Bill Miner, Stagecoach & Train Robber.* Surrey, B.C.: Heritage House Publishing, 1982.

Atwood, Kay, and Dennis Gray. *As Long as the World Goes On: The Land and People of Southwestern Oregon.* Portland: The Oregon History Project, Oregon Historical Society, 2005.

Bartlett, Grace. *From the Wallowas.* Enterprise, Ore.: Pika Press, 1992.

Berland, Sidney. "Harry Tracy." Columbia, Washington State Historical Society, Summer 1994, pp. 39–44.

Blakely, James, and Herbert Lundy. "When the Juniper Trees Bore Fruit." *Portland Oregonian*, March 12, 19, and 26, 1939.

Braly, David. *Juniper Empire: Early Days in Eastern and Central Oregon.* Prineville, Ore.: American Media Co., 1976.

Brogan, Phil. *East of the Cascades.* Portland, Ore.: Binford & Mort, 1971.

Capi, Lynn. "1923 Botched Train Holdup Nears Anniversary." *Statesman-Journal*, October 7, 2003.

Chipman, Art. *Tunnel 13.* Medford, Ore.: Pine Cone Publishers, 1977.

Churchill, E. Richard. *The McCartys.* Leadville, Colo.: Timberline Books, 1972.

Claeyssens, Paul G., and Ward Tonsfeldt. *Central Oregon: Adaptation & Compromise in an Arid Landscape.* Portland, Ore.: The Oregon History Project, Oregon Historical Society, 2005.

Collins, William, and Bruce Leven. *Black Bart: The True Story of the West's Most Famous Stagecoach Robber.* Mendocino, Calif.: Pacific Transcriptions, 1992.

Crook County Historical Society. "Reign of the Vigilantes." Pamphlets #44 and #58, Bowman Museum, Prineville, Ore.

Crook County Historical Society. "Sheep and Cattle Wars." Pamphlets #57 and #141, Bowman Museum, Prineville, Ore.

DeAutremont, Ray. "Ray DeAutremont's Confession." June 23, 1927.

Dugan, Mark, and John Boessenecker. *The Grey Fox: The True Story of Bill Miner, Last of the Old-Time Bandits*. Norman: University of Oklahoma Press, 1992.

Finn, John D. "Bandits' stolen gold still missing." *News-Register*, McMinnville, Ore.: July 6, 2011.

Flewelling, Stan. "The Dauntless Desperado: Harry Tracy." *White River Journal*, April 1998.

Gaddis, Thomas. "He Lived—He Died—For Hate." *Coronet*, March 1957, pp. 128–132.

Gaddis, Thomas E., and James O. Long. *Panzram, A Journal of Murder*. Los Angeles: Amok Books, 2002.

Gulick, Bill. *Manhunt: The Pursuit of Harry Tracy*. Caldwell, Idaho: Caxton Press, 1999.

Highberger, Mark. *Snake River Massacre*. Wallowa, Ore.: Bear Creek Press, 2000.

Hoeper, George. *Black Bart: Boulevardier Bandit*. Fresno, Calif.: World Dancer Press, 1995.

Horner, John Harley. "The Horner Papers." Wallowa County Historical Society.

Howard, John, and Larry Sturholm. *All for Nothing*. Portland, Ore.: Metropolitan Printing Co., 1976.

———. "Jim Blakely, Pioneer Sheriff of Crook County, Dies at 100 Years of Age," Obituary. *College Place (Wash.) Tribune*, January 29, 1953.

———. "Harry Tracy: King of the Western Robbers." *Portland Oregonian*, July 23, 1947.

———. "The State Penitentiary" *Daily Oregon Statesman*, January 1, 1907.

———. "Milton Bank Robbery" *Morning (Baker City) Democrat*, November 11, 1893.

Joers, Lawrence E. C. "Passenger on Number 13." *Oregon*, January 1980 pp. 125–30.

Kramer, George. "Mining in Southwestern Oregon: A Historic Context Statement." Eugene, Ore.: Heritage Research Associates Report No. 234, December 1999.

Mackay, Dean. "The Outlaw PO8." *Frontier Times*, Fall 1958, pp. 6–11.

Mackey, William. "Sailor Diggings, Pioneer Town of Gold Production." *Daily Courier*. Grants Pass, Ore.: February 6, 2006.

McArthur, Lewis A. *Oregon Geographic Names*. Portland: Oregon Historical Society Press, 1982.

McArthur, Lewis A., and Lewis L. McArthur. *Oregon Geographic Names*. Portland: Oregon Historical Society Press, 2003.

McCarthy, Linda. *A History of Oregon Sheriffs, 1841–1991*. Portland: Oregon Sheriffs Association, Taylor Publishing Company, 1992.

McCully, J. D. "Letter to his mother regarding the First Joseph Bank robbery." October 2, 1896. Joseph, Ore.: Wallowa County Historical Society.

Meier, Gary and Gloria. *Oregon Outlaws*. Boise, Idaho: Tamarack Books, 1996.

Nokes, R. Gregory. "Chinese Massacre Map," Chinese Historical Society Bulletin, November–December 2004. Chinese Historical Society of America, San Francisco.

Oregon Department of Corrections, "The Last Days of Superintendent Minto."

Oregon Department of Corrections, "Prison History of the Oregon State Penitentiary."

Oregon Sheriff's Archives, Benton County.

Oregon Sheriff's Archives, Grant County.

Oregon Sheriff's Archives, Harney County.

Oregon Sheriff's Archives, Jackson County.

Oregon Sheriff's Archives, Malheur County.

Oregon Sheriff's Archives, Marion County.

Oregon Sheriff's Archives, Umatilla County.

Oregon State Archives, "Carl Panzram Oregon State Penitentiary Case File."

Oregon State Archives. "Oregon Blue Book." Salem, Ore., 2011.

Personal communication, Gary Dielman, curator, Baker County Library, Baker County Historical Society, Baker City, Ore.

Peterson del Mar, David. *The World Rushed In: Northeastern Oregon.* Portland: The Oregon History Project, Oregon Historical Society, 2005.

Pintarich, Dick. "The Great Jailbreak." *Oregon,* December 1983– January 1984, pp. 95–103.

Rautenstrauch, Bill. "A Skeleton in the Closet." *Wallowa County Chieftan,* Enterprise, Ore., February 16, 1995.

Salem Public Library, "Salem Online History."

Sauerwein, Stan. *Gentleman Train Robber: The Daring Escapades of Bill Miner.* Canmore, Alberta: Altitude Publishing Canada, 2005.

Skovlin, Jon M., and Donna McDaniel. *In Pursuit of the McCartys.* Cove, Ore.: Reflections Publishing Co., 2001.

———. *Hank Vaughan.* Cove, Ore.: Reflections Publishing Co., 1996.

Stratton, David H. "The Snake River Massacre of Chinese Miners, 1887," *A Taste of the West.* Boulder, Colo.: Pruett Publishing Co., 1983.

Street, Willard, and Elsie Willard. *Sailors' Diggings.* Wilderville, Ore.: Wilderville Press, 1973.

Swallow, Richard. "The Strange Story of the World's Worst Murderer." *Master Detective,* February 1933, pp 49–52, 79

Warren, Larry. "Oregon's Legendary Sheriff." *Frontier Times,* October–November 1973, pp. 6–9.

Washington Sheriff's Archives, King County.

Webber, Bert. *Oregon's Great Train Holdup.* Fairfield, Wash.: Ye Galleon Press, 1973.

Wells, Fargo. "Wells, Fargo Since 1952." Wells, Fargo Museum.

Index

A

Albany, Oregon, 134
Albert, Chief, 48
Astoria, Oregon, 124, 128
Auburn, Oregon, 15, 105
Ayer, Joseph William, 38

B

Baker County, Oregon, 78, 79
Baldwin, Jeff. *See* Panzram, Carl
Bank of Astoria, 128
Barnes, George, 29
Barnes, Mossy, 24, 29
Barrett, Ollie, 59, 61
Bate, La, 119
Bates, Sidney L., 7, 9, 10
Beaudoin, Peter, 92, 98, 99
Belcrest Memorial Cemetery, 14
Benson, J. J., 133
Benton County Sheriff's
     Department, 123
Biggs, Alonzo, 73
Blachley, A. T., 89
Black Bart, 33, 35, 36, 38, 39, 40, 140
Blakely, James, 27
Blakely, Jim, 17, 26, 27, 28, 110
Blue Front Saloon, 109
Blue Mountains Forest Reserve, 51
Boles, Charles. *See* Black Bart
Brannan, Sam, 140
Breese, E. E., 77
Brichoux, Dave, 122
Brown, Ben J., 121
Brown, James, 93, 94, 96, 98
Bunten, Dick, 104
Burmeister's Saloon, 20
Burns, J. V., 128
Burns, Oregon, 102

C

California Stage Company, 31
Canfield, T. J. "Tigh," 115, 117,
     119, 120
Canyon City, Oregon, 103, 115
Carson, E. M., 74
Case, John, 57
Cassidy, Butch, 70, 79, 81
Cassidy, Dan, 80
Centerville, Oregon, 109
Central Oregon Wool Growers
     Association, 49
Chase, George, 37, 39
China Bar, Oregon, 118
Chinese Consul, 118
Chinese Exclusion Act, 115
Chinese Massacre Cove, 120
Chinese Massacre of 1887, 115
Chinese Six Companies, 118
Citizens Protective Union, 27
Civil War, 34
Clarnie, Oregon, 57
Collins, 123
Combs, John, 27
Concord Coach, 37
Conde, Porter, 88
Congleton, Billie, 45
Conn, J. C., 50
Cooper, Fred, 144, 145
Cordano, Detective, 72
Courtney, Sam, 45
Craig, George, 112, 118
Crook County, Oregon, 21, 24,
     27, 29, 48
Crooks, A. H., 16
Cutting, George, 48

D

Damrose, George, 124
DeAutremont, Belle, 3, 5
DeAutremont, Hugh, 2, 3, 5, 6,
     7, 8, 9, 11, 12, 13, 14
DeAutremont, Paul, 3
DeAutremont, Ray, 2, 3, 4, 5, 6,
     7, 8, 9, 10, 11, 13, 14
DeAutremont, Roy, 2, 3, 4, 5, 6,
     7, 8, 9, 12, 13, 14

Index

DeAutremont, Verne, 12
Dick Graham Saloon, 24
Donnely, Alex, 97
Dougherty, Elvyn E., 7, 8
Dug Bar, Oregon, 112, 115
Durbin, Frank W., 65, 73, 75

E

Eddings, Nort, 39
Enterprise, Oregon, 81, 82
Eugene, Oregon, 5, 6
Evans, Bruce, 115, 117, 118, 119
Express Ranch, 104

F

False Face Bandits, 71, 72
Falwell, Bill, 109, 110
Fargo, William, 36
Farr Brothers Lumber Company, 55, 58
Ferrell, F. B., 67
First Bank of Joseph, 93, 95, 98, 99
Fitzhugh, Cyrus, 93, 94, 96, 97, 99
Ford, Detective, 72
Foren, W. C., 19
Forepaugh's Circus, 87
Forsythe, E. J., 97
Frazier, Rush, 102
French, Peter, 102, 103

G

Gardner, J. C., 130
Gardner Shackle, 130
Gee, Heop, 119
Gervais, Oregon, 73, 74, 75
Girardet, Sheriff, 90
Glaze, Til, 27, 102, 107
Glick, Solomon, 60
Goble, Oregon, 55, 58
gold rush, 30, 31, 36, 136, 137
Gold Special, 2, 5
Goodwin, R. C., 121, 122
Graham, Dick, 108

Grant County, Oregon, 44
Greer, T., 74
Grey Fox. See Miner, Bill
Griffin, Eliza A., 123
Grindstone, Oregon, 41
Grizzly Mountain, 16

H

Haffney, Hugh, 7, 8
Harney Valley, Oregon, 15
Harrison, W. H., 18, 19, 21, 23, 26
Harshman, Guy, 52
Harshman, Z. G., 55, 56, 57, 58, 59, 60, 62, 63
Hart, O. J., 104
Hayes, Rutherford, 40
Headspot, William, 103
Hearn, Miles, 143
Heim, Sing, 119
Heinrich, Edward, 11
Hells Canyon, 112, 113, 115
Helm, Boone, 141
Heulet, Still, 106
Higgins, C. R., 128
Hoehn, Charles, 57, 58, 59, 60, 62, 63
Holmes, W. R., 82, 83
Homestead Act, 17
Hooker, Otto, 133, 134
Hotel Warshaur, 84, 86
Hughes, Carl, 115, 118, 119
Hume, James, 40
Humphrey, Charles, 124
Humphrey, George, 124
Huston, Sidney, 20, 21
Hyatt, G. W., 83
Hyde, John, 48

I

Industrial Workers of the World, 4
Inghram, Frank, 68, 77
Inland Sheep Shooters, 45, 47, 50, 51
Invincible Three, 83
Izee Sheep Shooters, 44, 45, 48, 50

Index

J

Jackson County, Oregon, 14
Jackson House Hotel, 18, 21
Jacksonville Democratic Times, 39
Jacksonville, Oregon, 31
Janes, J. T., 72
Jennings, Ralph, 14
Jim, Ah, 119
Joers, Lawrence E. C., 10
Johnson, Charles Orin "Coyle," 8, 9
Johnson, Walter, 133, 134
Jones, S., 68
Jordan, Frank, 15
Jory, Stephen, 16
Josephine County, Oregon, 136,
    144, 148
Joseph, Oregon, 91, 93
Joseph State Bank, 91, 98

K

Kane, William, 102
Kelly's Saloon, 24
King, August, 74
King, William, 124
Korner, Fred, 60

L

Lamb, Charity, 122, 123
Lamb, Mary Ann, 123
Lamb, Nathaniel, 122, 123
Langdon, Lucius, 17, 19, 21, 26
LaRue, Homer, 115, 117, 118, 119, 120
Lee, Hee, 119
Lee, Ye, 119
Lim, Heim, 119
Long, A. J., 134
Long, Charley, 29, 107, 108
Luckey, J. L., 17, 19
Luckey, John, 22
Luster, Charles, 20, 21

M

Maddock, Frank, 104
Marrett, J. O., 1, 8, 10

Martin, John, 93, 96, 97
Martin's Saloon, 93
Maupin, Garrett, 16
Maynard, Hiram, 115, 118, 119,
    120
McCarty, Bill, 78, 79, 80, 81, 82,
    83, 84, 85, 86, 88, 89
McCarty, Eck, 80
McCarty, Fred, 80, 84, 87, 88, 89
McCarty Gang, 81, 83, 87, 88,
    89, 90, 93
McCarty, George, 78, 79, 80, 84,
    86, 88, 90
McCarty, Lettie, 80
McCarty, Lois, 79, 80, 106, 111
McCarty, Matt, 80
McCarty, Nellie, 79, 80, 86, 90
McCarty, Pearl, 80
McCarty, Tom, 78, 79, 80, 81,
    82, 83, 84, 85, 88, 89, 90
McCully, J. D., 94, 95, 96
McDaniels, Frank, 102
McMillan, Robert, 115, 118, 119,
    120
Merrill, Dave, 66, 67, 68, 69, 70,
    72, 73, 75, 76, 77
Miner, Bill, 52, 53, 54, 55, 57, 58,
    59, 60, 62, 63, 64
Minnesota State Training School,
    125, 127
Minto, Harry, 132, 133, 134
Moffat, David, 80
Montana State Reform School,
    128
Montgomery, Jack, 32
Moody, Bill, 106
Moody, Z. F., 23
Moonshiners, 27
Morgan, Frank, 24
Morgan, Mike, 24
Morning Oregonian, 49
Mount Crest, 6, 11
Mullins, C. W., 128
Multnomah County Sheriff's
    Department, 62, 63

Index

N

Neese, T. Clay, 27
Nevins, James, 62
Noe, Lee, 121
Northern Pacific Railroad, 110

O

O'Brien, Oregon, 136, 138, 147, 148
O'Leary, John. *See* Panzram, Carl
Oliver, Ed, 102, 103
Olson, Ole, 124
Oregon and California Stage Coach
    Line, 32
Oregon Boot, 131, 132
Oregon National Guard, 74
Oregon Railway and Navigation
    Company, 57, 59
Oregon State Penitentiary, 14, 65,
    66, 67, 72, 77, 92, 98, 105,
    110, 130, 132, 135
Overland Mail Company, 37
Ownbey, Ben, 93, 94, 96, 97

P

Paiute Indians, 48
Panzram, Carl, 124, 125, 126,
    127, 128, 131, 132, 133, 134
Panzram, John, 125
Panzram, Lizzie, 125, 127
Patterson, Ferd, 141, 142
Patterson, Newton I., 124
Paulina, Chief, 16
Paulina, Oregon, 41, 44, 45
Pendleton East Oregonian, 108
Pendleton, Oregon, 111
Pinkerton agency, 62
placer mining, 138, 139
Plummer, Henry, 142
Pony Express, 37
Poole, Jim, 57
Portland Morning Oregonian, 26
Portland, Oregon, 70, 71, 130
Portland Oregonian, 66

Powder River Valley, 81, 89
Powell, Fred, 45
Price, James C., 13
Prineville, Oregon, 16, 18, 23, 26,
    27, 29, 50, 107, 108
Prineville Review, 49
Proebstel, Minnie, 92, 98

R

range wars, 41, 42, 43, 44, 45, 46,
    47, 49, 50, 51
Rawley, Neil, 77
Raymond, Charles, 77
Reynolds, Thomas, 13
Rinehart, H. C., 83
Roberts, J. W., 73
Robie, Martha, 111
Robinson Gulch, 116, 117, 118
Rogue River Indian War, 27, 138,
    139
Ross (guard), 69

S

Sailors' Diggings, 136, 137, 138,
    139, 140, 141, 142, 143,
    144, 146, 147, 148
Salem, Oregon, 4, 14, 66, 72, 73, 130
San Quentin State Prison, 53
Sara Jane, 88
7 U Ranch, 87, 88
Scott, Harvey, 26
Seattle Daily Times, 75
See, Wy, 119
Selby, George, 124
Seng, Marvin L., 7, 9
Shadows, 14
Shaniko, Oregon, 42
Sheahan, D. W., 83
Sherman, William Tecumseh, 35,
    40
Shine, John, 33
Shorty Davis, 23
Simpson, W. Ray, 89

Index

Sing, Hop, 119
Siskiyou Mountains, 5, 31, 33, 35, 40, 140
Siskiyou Pass, 1, 5, 40
Siskiyou Summit, 38
Smith, Fred, 41
Smith, Sam, 27
Snodgrass, Henry, 44, 45
Southern Pacific Railroad Company, 1, 3, 5, 6, 10, 13, 56
Spanish Tom, 15, 16
Sparta, Oregon, 85
Staats, Steve, 23
stagecoach robbery, 30, 31, 32, 33, 34, 39, 40, 55, 140
Stenger, Pete, 102
Stevenson, H. F., 59
Storey, William, 62
Stover, Chris, 144
Summerville, Oregon, 83
Sundance Kid, 70
Sutter, John, 136
Swartz, Al, 20, 21

T

Teal & Coleman Ranch, 42
Terry, Jake, 63, 64
Thompson, S. G., 23
Thompson, William "Bud," 17, 20, 23, 24, 25, 26, 29
Tiffany, B. F., 69
Tom the Spaniard, 105
Tracy, Harry, 66, 67, 68, 69, 70, 71, 72, 73, 74, 75, 76, 77
Tracy, Mollie, 67, 72
train robbery, 52, 55, 56, 57, 61, 63, 84
Triskett Gang, 136, 143, 144, 146, 147, 148
Triskett, Henry, 143
Triskett, Jack, 143
Tri-Weekly Statesman, 15
Tucker, Dave, 91, 92, 94, 95, 96, 97, 98, 99

U

Umatilla Indian Reservation, 111
Union Pacific Railroad, 84

V

Vaughan, Frank, 115, 116, 117, 118
Vaughan, Hank, 80, 84, 101, 103, 104, 107, 108, 109, 110, 111
vigilantes, 15, 16, 19, 20, 21, 24, 26, 27, 29, 105, 107
Vincent, F. K., 118

W

Wagner, Fred, 96, 98
Wagner, J. P., 108
Waldo, Oregon, 138, 143, 144, 148
Wallowa County, Oregon, 78, 91
Wallowa National Bank, 81, 82
Warner, Matt, 79, 80, 81, 82, 83, 84, 85, 88, 90
Warner, Rose, 88
Warnke, Robert, 135
Wasco County, Oregon, 42, 44
Weiner, Detective, 72
Wellman, Mary Jane, 63
Wells, Fargo & Company, 32, 34, 35, 36, 37, 38, 40
Wells, George, 143
Wells, Henry, 36
Wey, Albert, 72
Wild Bunch, 70, 79, 81
Willamette Valley, 137
Winckler, Gus A., 23, 26
Withycombe, James, 132
Wright, Harry, 72

Y

Yee, Hee, 119

About the Author

Jim Yuskavitch has worked as a freelance writer and photographer since 1993. His other books include *Fishing Oregon, Oregon Wildlife Viewing Guide, Mysteries and Legends Oregon, Quick Casts: Portland, Oregon,* and *Oregon Nature Weekends.* He is also the coauthor of *The Insiders' Guide to Bend and Central Oregon.* He lives in Sisters, Oregon.